AF344303

HIT THE MARK

SANGAM TEXTS

GENERAL EDITOR

RAGHAVAN IYER

Sangam Texts are aids to contemplation and action, the creative fusion of theoria *(sankhya)* and praxis *(yoga)*. In the ancient world, before the proliferation of print, emphasis was given to exemplification. Remarkable individuals emerged from time to time to bear witness to the authentic transcendence of social roles and codes and traditional structures. The supreme ideal of the *Jivanmukta*, the truly free man or woman, was emulated even by householders through the practice of renunciation *(sannyasa)*. Furthermore, the *ashrama* ideal was kept alive, in diverse ways, by aspirants who assumed monastic modes of life and adopted self-binding vows. In the Aquarian Age, the shared ideal of secular monasticism is pertinent to all those who wish to explore fresh and feasible ways of achieving self-regeneration in the service of *Lokasangraha*, the welfare of the whole of humanity. The thoughtful writings in this series span the mystical and the practical, the timeless and the timely, giving a basis for lifelong reflection and self-transcendence.

SANGAM TEXTS

HIT THE MARK

Hit the Mark contains twenty-four pithy essays on living the spiritual life by William Quan Judge, co-founder of the modern Theosophical Movement. "Aum", "The Udgitha" and "A Commentary on the Gayatri" point to the profound significance of the most sacred invocations in the Hindu tradition. "Our Sun and the True Sun" and "The Allegorical Umbrella" convey the richness and relevance of two ancient symbols. "Meditation, Concentration, Will", "Hit the Mark" and "Rules in Occultism" provide invaluable guidance to the seeker of spiritual wisdom. "The Dweller of the Threshold", " 'Forms' of Elementals" and "Astral Intoxication" alert the aspirant to hazards and pitfalls on the path towards enlightenment. "Mental Discipline" indicates the requirements for real knowledge, and "Mantrams" illustrates the potency of sound. The universality of *Theosophia* is stressed in "Universal Applications of Doctrine", followed by a warning against "Mechanical Theosophy". "Advantages and Disadvantages in Life", "How Should We Treat Others?", "Am I My Brother's Keeper?" and "Friends or Enemies in the Future" deal with ethical implications of karma and reincarnation. "On the Future: A Few Reflections" and "Musings on the True Theosophist's Path" offer telling insights into metahistory and mystical self-training. "Mahatmas As Ideals and Facts" and "Guru and Chela" consider the responsibilities of discipleship and the reality of the arcane brotherhood of adepts. The book concludes with "The Tell-Tale Picture Gallery", a thought-provoking allegory of the spiritual quest.

HIT THE MARK

WILLIAM Q. JUDGE

To render the priceless privilege of noetic insight relevant in daily life requires strength of concentration, serenity of feeling and skill in action.

HERMES

CONCORD GROVE PRESS

1985

CONCORD GROVE PRESS
London   Santa Barbara   New York

First Edition: December 21, 1985

ISBN 0-88695-024-4

10 9 8 7 6 5 4 3 2 1

CONTENTS

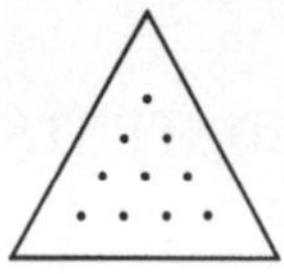

In the first place revere the Immortal Gods, as they
are established and ordained by the Law.

Reverence the Oath. In the next place revere the
Heroes who are full of goodness and light.

Honour likewise the Terrestrial Daimons by
rendering them the worship lawfully due to them.

PYTHAGORAS

*We have to educate the West so that it may appreciate
the possibilities of the East, and thus on the waiting structure
in the East may be built up a new order of things for the
benefit of the whole. We have, each one of us, to make
ourselves a centre of light — a picture gallery from which
shall be projected on the astral light such scenes, such
influences, such thoughts, as may influence many for good,
shall thus arouse a new current, and then finally result in
drawing back the great and the good from other spheres,
from beyond the earth.*

W. Q. JUDGE

WILLIAM QUAN JUDGE

(April 13, 1851 — March 21, 1896)

AUM

The most sacred mystic syllable of the Vedas is Aum. It is the first letter of the Sanskrit alphabet, and by some it is thought to be the sound made by a new born child when the breath is first drawn into the lungs. The daily prayers of the Hindu Brahmin are begun and ended with it, and the ancient sacred books say that with that syllable the gods themselves address the most Holy One.

In the Chandogya Upanishad its praises are sung in these words: *

> Let a man meditate on the syllable OM called the udgitha,†
> .. it is the best of all essences, the highest, deserving the
> highest place, the eighth.

It is then commanded to meditate on this syllable as the breath, of two kinds, in the body — the vital breath and the mere breath in the mouth or lungs, for by this meditation come knowledge and proper performance of sacrifice. In verse 10 is found: "Now, therefore, it would seem to follow that both he who knows the true meaning of OM, and he who does not, perform the same sacrifice. But this is not so, for knowledge and ignorance are different. The sacrifice which a man performs with knowledge, faith, and the Upanishad is more powerful."

Outwardly the same sacrifice is performed by both, but that performed by him who has knowledge, and has meditated on the secret meaning of OM partakes of the qualities inhering in OM, which need just that knowledge and faith as the medium through which they may become visible and active. If a jeweler and a mere ploughman sell a precious stone, the knowledge of the former bears better fruit than the ignorance of the latter.

Shankaracharya in his *Sharir Bhashya* dwells largely on OM, and in the *Vayu Purana,* a whole chapter is devoted to it. Now as Vayu is air, we can see in what direction the minds of those who were

---

* Khandogya Upanishad, 1st Khanda. See Vol. 1, *Sacred Books of the East.* Müller.

† Hymn of Praise to Brahm.

concerned with that purana were tending. They were analyzing sound, which will lead to discoveries of interest regarding the human spiritual and physical constitution. In sound is tone, and tone is one of the most important and deep reaching of all natural things. By tone, the natural man, and the child, express the feelings, just as animals in their tones make known their nature. The tone of the voice of the tiger is quite different from that of the dove, as different as their natures are from each other, and if the sights, sounds, and objects in the natural world mean anything, or point the way to any laws underlying these differences, then there is nothing puerile in considering the meaning of tone.

The Padma Purana says: "The syllable OM is the leader of all prayers. Let it therefore be employed in the beginning of all prayers," and Manu, in his laws ordains: "A Brahmin, at the beginning and end of a lesson on the Vedas, must always pronounce the syllable OM, for unless OM precede, his learning will slip away from him, and unless it follows, nothing will be long retained."

The celebrated Hindoo Raja, Ramohun Roy, in a treatise on this letter says:

> OM, when considered as one letter, uttered by the help of one articulation, is the symbol of the Supreme Spirit. 'One letter (OM) is the emblem of the Most High, Manu II, 83.' But when considered as a triliteral word consisting of a, u, m, it implies the three *Vedas*, the three *states* of human nature, the three *divisions* of the universe, and the three *deities* — Brahma, Vishnu and Siva, agents in the *creation*, *preservation* and *destruction* of this world; or, properly speaking, the three principal attributes of the Supreme Being personified in those three deities. In this sense it implies, in fact, the universe controlled by the Supreme Spirit.

Now we may consider that there is pervading the whole universe a single homogeneous resonance, sound, or tone, which acts, so to speak, as the awakener, or vivifying power, stirring all the molecules into action. This is what is represented in all languages by the vowel *a*, which takes precedence of all others. This is the word, the *verbum*, the *Logos* of St. John of the Christians, who says: "In the beginning was the Word, and the word was with God, and the word was God."* This is creation, for without this resonance or motion among the quiescent particles, there would be no visible universe. That is to say, upon sound, or as the Aryans called it, *Nada Brahma* (divine resonance), depends the evolution of the visible from the invisible.

But this sound *a*, being produced, at once alters itself into *au*, so that the second sound, *u*, is that one made by the first in continuing its existence. The vowel *u*, which in itself is a compound one, therefore represents preservation. And the idea of preservation is contained also in creation, or evolution, for there could not be anything to preserve, unless it had first come into existence.

If these two sounds, so compounded into one, were to proceed indefinitely, there would be of course no destruction of them. But it is not possible to continue the utterance further than the breath, and whether the lips are compressed, or the tongue pressed against the roof of the mouth, or the organs behind that used, there will be in the finishing of the utterance the closure or *m* sound, which among the Aryans had the meaning of *stoppage*. In this last letter there is found the destruction of the whole word or letter. To reproduce it a slight experiment will show that by no possibility can it be begun with *m*, but that *au* invariably commences even the utterance of *m* itself. Without fear of successful contradiction, it can be asserted that all speech begins with *au*, and the ending or destruction of speech is in *m*.

The word "tone" is derived from the Latin and Greek words meaning sound and tone. In the Greek the word "tonos" means a "stretching" or "straining." As to the character of the sound, the word "tone" is used to express all varieties, such as high, low, grave, acute, sweet and harsh sounds. In music it gives the peculiar quality of that sound produced, and also distinguishes one instrument from another; as rich tone, reedy tone, and so on. In medicine it designates the state of the body, but is there used more in the signification of strength, and refers to strength or tension. It is not difficult to connect the use of the word in medicine with the divine resonance of which we spoke, because we may consider tension to be the vibration, or quantity of vibration, by which sound is apprehended by the ear, and if the whole

---

* St. John, C. 1, V. 1.

system gradually goes down so that its tone is lowered without stoppage, the result will at last be dissolution for that collection of molecules. In painting, the tone also shows the general drift of the picture, just as it indicates the same thing in morals and manners. We say, "a low tone of morals, an elevated tone of sentiment, a courtly tone of manners," so that tone has a signification which is applied universally to either good or bad, high or low. And the only letter which we can use to express it, or symbolize it, is the *a* sound, in its various changes, long, short and medium. And just as the *tone* of manners, of morals, of painting, of music, means the real character of each, in the same way the tones of the various creatures, including man himself, mean or express the real character; and altogether joined in the deep murmur of nature, go to swell the *Nada Brahma,* or Divine resonance, which at last is heard as the music of the spheres.

Meditation on tone, as expressed in this Sanscrit word OM, will lead us to a knowledge of the secret Doctrine. We find expressed in the merely mortal music the seven divisions of the divine essence, for as the microcosm is the little copy of the macrocosm, even the halting measures of man contain the little copy of the whole, in the seven tones of the octave. From that we are led to the seven colors, and so forward and upward to the Divine radiance which is the Aum. For the Divine Resonance, spoken of above, is not the Divine Light itself. The Resonance is only the outbreathing of the first sound of the entire Aum.

This goes on during what the Hindoos call a Day of Brahma, which, according to them, lasts a thousand ages. It manifests itself not only as the power which stirs up and animates the particles of the Universe, but also in the evolution and dissolution of man, of the animal and mineral kingdom, and of solar systems. Among the Aryans it was represented in the planetary system by Mercury, who has always been said to govern the intellectual faculties, and to be the universal stimulator. Some old writers have said that it is shown through Mercury, amongst mankind, by the universal talking of women.

And wherever this Divine Resonance is closed or stopped by death or other change, the Aum has been uttered there. These utterances of Aum are only the numerous microscopic enunciations of the Word, which is uttered or completely ended, to use the

Hermetic or mystical style of language, only when the great Brahm stops the outbreathing, closes the vocalization by the *m* sound, and thus causes the universal dissolution. This universal dissolution is known in the Sanscrit and in the secret Doctrine, as the *Maha Pralaya, Maha* being "the great," and *Pralaya* "dissolution." And so, after thus arguing, the ancient Rishees of India said: "Nothing is begun or ended; everything is changed, and that which we call death is only a transformation." In thus speaking they wished to be understood as referring to the manifested universe, the so-called death of a sentient creature being only a transformation of energy, or a change of the mode and place of manifestation of the Divine Resonance. Thus early in the history of the race the doctrine of conservation of energy was known and applied. The Divine Resonance, or the *au* sound, is the universal energy, which is conserved during each Day of Brahma, and at the coming on of the great Night is absorbed again into the whole. Continually appearing and disappearing, it transforms itself again and again, covered from time to time by a veil of matter called its visible manifestation, and never lost, but always changing itself from one form to another. And herein can be seen the use and beauty of the Sanscrit. Nada Brahma is Divine Resonance; that is, after saying *Nada,* if we stopped with Brahm, logically we must infer that the *m* sound at the end of Brahm signified the Pralaya, thus confuting the position that the Divine Resonance existed, for if it had stopped it could not be resounding. So they added an *a* at the end of the Brahm, making it possible to understand that as *Brahma* the sound was still manifesting itself. But time would not suffice to go into this subject as it deserves and these remarks are only intended as a feeble attempt to point out the real meaning and purpose of Aum.

For the above reasons, and out of the great respect we entertain for the wisdom of the Aryans, was the symbol adopted and placed on the cover of this magazine and at the head of the text.

With us OM has a signification. It represents the constant undercurrent of meditation, which ought to be carried on by every man, even while engaged in the necessary duties of this life. There is for every conditioned being a target at which the aim is constantly directed. Even the very animal kingdom we do not except, for it, below us, awaits its evolution into a higher state; it

12

unconsciously perhaps, but nevertheless actually, aims at the same
target.

> Having taken the bow, the great weapon, let him place
> on it the arrow, sharpened by devotion. Then, having drawn
> it with a thought directed to that which is, hit the mark, O
> friend — the Indestructible. OM is the bow, the Self is the
> arrow, Brahman is called its aim. It is to be hit by a man
> who is not thoughtless; and then as the arrow becomes one
> with the target, he will become one with Brahman. Know
> him alone as the Self, and leave off other words. He is the
> bridge of the Immortal. Meditate on the Self as OM. Hail to
> you that you may cross beyond the sea of darkness.*

AUM!

The Path, April 1886

* Mundaka Upanishad, II, Kh. 2. (Müller's Tr.)

THE UDGITHA

OM is the Udgitha.
In the *Maitrayana-Brahmana-Upanishad,* (Pr. VI), it is said:

> The Udgitha, called Pranava, the leader, the bright, the sleepless, free from old age and death, three footed (waking, dream, and deep sleep), consisting of three letters and likewise to be known as fivefold, is placed in the cave of the heart.

This is the Self. Not the mere body or the faculties of the brain, but the Highest Self. And that must be meditated on, or worshipped, with a constant meditation. *Hymn of praise,* then, means that we accept the existence of that Self and aspire to or adore Him. Therefore, it is said again, in the same Upanishad:

> In the beginning Brahman was all this. He was one, and infinite.... The Highest Self is not to be fixed, he is unlimited, unborn, not to be reasoned about, not to be conceived. He is, like the ether, everywhere, and at the destruction of the Universe, he alone is awake. Thus from that ether he wakes all this world, which consists of (his) thought only, and by him alone is all this meditated on, and in him it is dissolved. His is that luminous form which shines in the sun, and the manifold light in the smokeless fire.... He who is in the fire, and he who is in the heart, and he who is in the sun, they *are one and the same.* He who knows this becomes one with the One.

Now, "to know" this, does not mean to merely apprehend the statement, but actually become personally acquainted with it by interior experience. And this is difficult. But it is to be sought after. And the first step to it is the attempt to realize universal brotherhood, for when one becomes identified with the One, who is all, he "participates in the souls of all creatures"; surely then the first step in the path is universal brotherhood.

14

The hymn of praise to Brahm (which is Brahman) is the real object of this magazine, and of our existence. The hymn is used, in the sacrifice, when verbally expressed, and we can offer it in our daily existence, in each act, whether eating, sleeping, waking, or in any state. A man can hardly incorporate this idea in his being and not be spiritually and morally benefitted.

The Path, May 1886

SVASAMVEDANA

I am neither earth nor fire, neither air nor ether, neither sensory powers nor all these together, as all of these are transient. I am He that remains alone in deep dreamless rest, the secondless, supreme and attributeless Bliss of Shiva.

I am neither caste nor its divisions, neither rite nor rule, nor am I the fixed mind or mood or mental exercise; this entire illusion of 'I' and 'mine' is rooted in the not-self and is wholly dispelled by the cognition of the Self. I am the secondless, supreme and attributeless Bliss of Shiva.

I am neither above nor below, neither inside nor outside, neither midward nor forward, neither before nor behind; I am indivisible and partless and all-pervading like space. I am the secondless, supreme and attributeless Bliss of Shiva.

Say not that It is One, as there can be no second, nothing other than That. There is neither uniqueness nor commonality, neither entity nor non-entity; this secondless One is neither void nor plenum. How can I convey this supreme wisdom?

SHRI SHANKARACHARYA

A COMMENTARY ON THE GAYATRI

*Unveil, O Thou who givest sustenance to the Universe,
from whom all proceed, to whom all must return, that face
of the True Sun now hidden by a vase of golden light, that
we may see the truth and do our whole duty on our journey
to thy sacred seat.* — The Gayatri

I have adopted a translation as above, which is excellent in its giving of the meaning of this verse. What is the Gayatri? It is the sacred verse of the Hindus and begins with Om, their sacred word and letter. Its first words are: *Om, Bhur, Bhuva, Svah.*

The first word [A U M] contains in it a declaration of the three periods of a Manvantara and the three powers of that great Being who alone Is. Of a manvantara it is the beginning, the middle, and the end, and the three powers are Creation (or manifesting), Preservation (or carrying on), and Destruction. The three first words, bhur, bhuva, svah, draw attention to and designate the three worlds. The whole verse is an aspiration in the highest sense. Every Brahman at his initiation is further instructed in this verse, but from giving that I am necessarily excused, as I cannot give it in a way in which I have not received it.

Unveil is the cry of the man who is determined to know the truth and who perceives that something hides it from him. It is hidden by his own Karmic effects, which have put him now where the brain and the desires are too strong for the higher self to pierce through so long as he remains careless and ignorant. The cry is not made to some man-made god with parts, passions, and attributes, but to the Self above who seeth in secret and bringeth out to light. It is directed to that on which the Universe is built and standeth, — no other than the Self which is in every man and which sitteth like a bird in a tree watching while another eats the fruit.

From this the whole Universe proceeds out into manifestation. The ancients held that all things whatsoever existed in fact solely in the idea, and therefore the practitioner of Yoga was taught — and soon discovered — that sun, moon, and stars were in himself, and until he learned this he could not proceed. This doctrine is very old, but today is adopted by many modern reasoners. For they perceive on reflection that no object enters the eye, and that whether we perceive through sight or feeling or any other sense whatever all objects are existing solely in idea. Of old this was demonstrated in two ways. First, by showing the disciple the actual interpenetration of one world by another. As that while we live here among those things called objective by us, other beings were likewise living in and among us and our objects and therein actually carrying on their avocations, perceiving the objects on their plane as objective, and wholly untouched by and insensible to us and the objects we think so material. This is no less true today than it was then. And if it were not true, modern hypnotism, clairvoyance, or clairaudience would be impossible. This was shown by a second method precisely similar to mesmeric and hypnotic experiments, only that to these was added the power to make the subject step aside from himself and with a dual consciousness note his own condition. For if a barrier of wood were erected in the sight of the subject which he clearly perceived and knew was wood, impervious to sight and an obstacle to movement, yet when hypnotized he saw it not, yet could perceive all objects behind it which were hidden in his normal state, and when he pressed against it thinking it to be empty air and feeling naught but force, he could not pass but wondered why the empty air restrained his body. This is modern and ancient. Clearly it demonstrates the illusionary nature of objectivity. The objectivity is only real relatively, for the mind sees no objects whatever but only their idea, and at present is conditioned through its own evolution until it shall have developed other powers and qualities.

The request made in the verse to *unveil the face of the True Sun* is that the Higher Self may shine down into us and do its work of illumination. This also spreads forth a natural fact unknown to moderns, which is that the Sun we see is not the true sun, and signifies too that the light of intellect is not the true sun of our moral being. Our forefathers in the dim past knew how to draw forth through the visible Sun the forces from the True one. We have temporarily forgotten this because our evolution and descent into the hell of matter, in order to save the whole, have interposed a screen. They say in Christian lands that Jesus went into hell for three days. This is correct, but not peculiar to Jesus. Humanity is doing this for three days, which is merely the mystical way of saying that we must descend into matter for three periods so immense in time that the logarithm of one day is given to each period. Logarithms were not first known to Napier, but were taught in the pure form of the mysteries, because alone by their use could certain vast calculations be made.

Which is now hidden by a vase of Golden Light. That is, the light of the True Sun — the Higher Self — is hidden by the blood contained in the vase of the mortal body. The blood has two aspects — not here detailed — in one of which it is a helper to perception, in the other a hindrance. But it signifies here the passions and desires, *Kama*, the personal self, the thirst for life. It is this that veils from us the true light. So long as desire and the personality remain strong, just so long will the light be blurred, so long will we mistake words for knowledge and knowledge for the thing we wish to know and to realize.

The *object* of this prayer is that we may carry out our whole duty, after becoming acquainted with the truth, while we are on our *journey to thy Sacred Seat*. This is our pilgrimage, not of one, not selfishly, not alone, but the whole of humanity. For the sacred seat is not the Brahmanical heaven of Indra, nor the Christian selfish heaven acquired without merit while the meritorious suffer the pains of hell. It is that place where all meet, where alone all are one. It is when and where the three great sounds of the first word of the prayer merge into one soundless sound. This is the only proper prayer, the sole saving aspiration.

The Path, January 1893

OUR SUN AND THE TRUE SUN

Considering how little is known of the sun of this system, it is not to be wondered at that still more is this the case respecting the true sun. Science laughs, of course, at the mystic's "true sun," for it sees none other than the one shining in the heavens. This at least they pretend to know, for it rises and sets each day and can be to some extent observed during eclipses or when spots appear on it, and with their usual audacity the 19th century astronomers learnedly declare all that they do not know about the mighty orb, relegating the ancient ideas on the subject to the limbo of superstitious nonsense. It is not to the modern schools that I would go for information on this subject, because in my opinion, however presumptuous it may seem, they really know but little about either Moon or Sun.

A dispute is still going on as to whether the sun *throws out heat.** On one hand it is asserted that he does; on the other, that the heat is produced by the combination of the forces from the sun with the elements on and around this earth. The latter would seem to the mystic to be true. Another difference of opinion exists among modern astronomers as to the distance of the sun from us, leaving the poor mystic to figure it out as he may. Even on the subject of spots on our great luminary, everything nowadays is mere conjecture. It is accepted hypothetically — and no more — that there may be a connection between those spots and electrical disturbances here. Some years ago Nasmyth discovered† objects (or changes) on the photosphere consisting of what he called "willow leaves," 1000 miles long and 300 miles broad, that constantly moved and appeared to be in shoals. But what are these? No one knows. Science can do no more about informing us than any keen sighted ordinary mortal using a fine telescope. And as to whether these "willow leaves" have any connection with the

---

* Among great scientists such as Newton, Secchi, Pouillet, Spaeren, Rosetti, and others, there is a difference as to estimated heat of the sun shown by their figures, for Pouillet says 1,461° and Waterston 9,000,000° or a variation of 8,998,600°!

† See *Source of Heat in the Sun*, R. Hunt, F.R.S. Pop. Sc. Rev. Vol. IV, p. 148.

spots or themselves have relation to earthly disturbances, there is equal silence. To sum it up, then, our scientific men know but little about the visible sun. A few things they must some day find out, such as other effects from sun spots than mere electrical disturbances; the real meaning of sun spots; the meaning of the peculiar color of the sun sometimes observed — such as that a few years ago attributed to "cosmic dust," for the want of a better explanation to veil ignorance; and a few other matters of interest.

But we say that this sun they have been examining is not the real one, nor any sun at all, but is only an appearance, a mere reflection to us of part of the true sun. And, indeed, we have some support even from modern astronomers, for they have begun to admit that our entire solar system is in motion around some far off undetermined centre which is so powerful that it attracts our solar orb and thus draws his entire system with him. But they know not if this unknown centre be a sun. They conjecture that it is, but will only assert that it is a centre of attraction for us. Now it may be simply a larger body, *or a stronger centre of energy*, than the sun, and in turn quite possibly it may be itself revolving about a still more distant and more powerful centre. In this matter the modern telescope and power of calculation are quickly baffled, because they very soon arrive at a limit in the starry field where, all being apparently stationary because of immense distances, there are no means of arriving at a conclusion. All these distant orbs may be in motion, and therefore it cannot be said where the true centre is. Your astronomer will admit that even the constellations in the Zodiac, immovable during ages past, may in truth be moving, but at such enormous and awful distances that for us they appear not to move.

My object, however, is to draw your attention to the doctrine that there is a true sun of which the visible one is a reflection, and that in this true one there is spiritual energy and help, just as our own beloved luminary contains the spring of our physical life and motion. It is useless now to speculate on which of the many stars in the heavens may be the real sun, for I opine it is none of them, since, as I said before, a physical centre of attraction for this system may only be a grade higher than ours, and the servant of a centre still farther removed. We must work in our several degrees, and it is not in our power to overleap one step in the chain that leads to the highest. Our own sun is, then, for us the symbol of the true one he reflects, and by meditating on "the most excellent light of the true sun" we can gain help in our struggle to assist humanity. Our physical sun is for physics, not metaphysics, while that true one shines down within us. The orb of day guards and sustains the animal economy; the true sun shines into us through its medium within our nature. We should then direct our thought to that true sun and prepare the ground within for its influence, just as we do the ground without for the vivifying rays of the King of Day.

The Path, February 1890   MARTTANDA

THE ALLEGORICAL UMBRELLA

In the Buddhist stories there are numerous references to umbrellas. When Buddha is said to have granted to his disciples the power of seeing what they called "Buddha Fields," they saw myriads of Buddhas sitting under trees and jewelled umbrellas. There are not wanting in the Hindu books and monuments references to and representations of umbrellas being held over personages. In a very curious and extremely old stone *relievo* at the Seven Pagodas in India, showing the conflict between Durga and the demons, the umbrella is figured over the heads of the Chiefs. It is not our intention to exalt this common and useful article to a high place in occultism, but we wish to present an idea in connection with it that has some value for the true student.

In the Upanishads we read the invocation: "Reveal, O Pushan, that face of the true sun which is now hidden by a golden lid." This has reference to the belief of all genuine occultists, from the earliest times to the present day, that there is a "true sun," and that the sun we see is a secondary one; or, to put it in plainer language, that there is an influence or power in the sun which may be used, if obtained by the mystic, for beneficent purposes, and which, if not guarded, hidden, or obscured by a cover, would work destruction to those who might succeed in drawing it out. This was well known in ancient Chaldea, and also to the old Chinese astronomers: the latter had certain instruments which they used for the purpose of concentrating particular rays of sunlight as yet unknown to modern science and now forgotten by the flowery land philosophers. So much for that sun we see, whose probable death is calculated by some aspiring scientists who deal in absurdities.

But there is the *true centre* of which the sun in heaven is a symbol and partial reflection. This centre let us place for the time with the Dhyan Chohans or planetary spirits. It is all knowing, and so intensely powerful that, were a struggling disciple to be suddenly introduced to its presence unprepared, he would be consumed, both body and soul. And this is the goal we are all striving after, and many of us asking to see even at the opening of the race. But for our protection a cover, or umbrella, has been placed beneath IT. The ribs are the Rishees, or Adepts, or Mahatmas; the Elder Brothers of the race. The handle is in every man's hand. And although each man is, or is to be, connected with some particular one of those Adepts, he can also receive the influence from the *true centre* coming down through the handle.

The light, life, knowledge, and power falling upon this cover permeate in innumerable streams the whole mass of men beneath, whether they be students or not. As the disciple strives upward, he begins to separate himself from the great mass of human beings, and becomes in a more or less definite manner connected with the ribs. Just as the streams of water flow down from the points of the ribs of our umbrellas, so the spiritual influences pour out from the adepts who form the frame of the protecting cover, without which poor humanity would be destroyed by the blaze from the spiritual world.

The Path, February 1890   **WILLIAM BREHON**

MEDITATION, CONCENTRATION, WILL

These three, meditation, concentration, will, have engaged the attention of Theosophists perhaps more than any other three subjects. A canvass of opinions would probably show that the majority of our reading and thinking members would rather hear these subjects discussed and read definite directions about them than any others in the entire field. They say they must meditate, they declare a wish for concentration, they would like a powerful will, and they sigh for strict directions, readable by the most foolish theosophist. It is a western cry for a curriculum, a course, a staked path, a line and rule by inches and links. Yet the path has long been outlined and described, so that any one could read the directions whose mind had not been half-ruined by modern false education, and memory rotted by the superficial methods of a superficial literature and a wholly vain modern life.

Let us divide Meditation into two sorts. First is the meditation practiced at a set time, or an occasional one, whether by design or from physiological idiosyncrasy. Second is the meditation of an entire lifetime, that single thread of intention, intentness, and desire running through the years stretching between the cradle and the grave. For the first, in Patanjali's Aphorisms will be found all needful rules and particularity. If these are studied and not forgotten, then practice must give results. How many of those who reiterate the call for instructions on this head have read that book, only to turn it down and never again consider it? Far too many.

The mysterious subtle thread of a life meditation is that which is practiced every hour by philosopher, mystic, saint, criminal, artist, artisan, and merchant. It is pursued in respect to that on which the heart is set; it rarely languishes; at times the meditating one greedily running after money, fame, and power looks up briefly and sighs for a better life during a brief interval, but the passing flash of a dollar or a sovereign recalls him to his modern senses, and the old meditation begins again. Since all theosophists are here in the social whirl I refer to, they can every one take these words to themselves as they please. Very certainly, if their life meditation is fixed low down near the ground, the results flowing to them from it will be strong, very lasting, and related to the low level on which they work. Their semi-occasional meditations will give precisely semi-occasional results in the long string of recurring births.

"But then," says another, "what of concentration? We must have it. We wish it; we lack it." Is it a piece of goods that you can buy it, do you think, or something that will come to you just for the wishing? Hardly. In the way we divided meditation into two great sorts, so we can divide concentration. One is the use of an already acquired power on a fixed occasion, the other the deep and constant practice of a power that has been made a possession. Concentration is not memory, since the latter is known to act without our concentrating on anything, and we know that centuries ago the old thinkers very justly called memory a phantasy. But by reason of a peculiarity of the human mind the associative part of memory is waked up the very instant concentration is attempted. It is this that makes students weary and at last drives them away from the pursuit of concentration. A man sits down to concentrate on the highest idea he can formulate, and like a flash troops of recollections of all sorts of affairs, old thoughts and impressions come before his mind, driving away the great object he first selected, and concentration is at an end.

This trouble is only to be corrected by practice, by assiduity, by continuance. No strange and complicated directions are needed. All we have to do is to try and to keep on trying.

The subject of the Will has not been treated of much in theosophical works, old or new. Patanjali does not go into it at all. It seems to be inferred by him through his aphorisms. Will is universal, and belongs to not only man and animals, but also to every other natural kingdom. The good and bad man alike have will, the child and the aged, the wise and the lunatic. It is therefore a power devoid in itself of moral quality. That quality must be added by man.

So the truth must be that will acts according to desire, or, as the older thinkers used to put it, "behind will stands desire." This is why the child, the savage, the lunatic, and the wicked man so often exhibit a stronger will than others. The wicked man has intensified his desires, and with that his will. The lunatic has but few desires, and draws all his will force into these; the savage is free from convention, from the various ideas, laws, rules, and suppositions to which the civilized person is subject, and has nothing to distract his will. So to make our will strong we must have fewer desires. Let those be high, pure, and altruistic; they will give us strong will.

No mere practice will develop will *per se*, for it exists forever, fully developed in itself. But practice will develop in us the power to call on that will which is ours. Will and Desire lie at the doors of Meditation and Concentration. If we desire truth with the same intensity that we had formerly wished for success, money, or gratification, we will speedily acquire meditation and possess concentration. If we do all our acts, small and great, every moment, for the sake of the whole human race, as representing the Supreme Self, then every cell and fibre of the body and inner man will be turned in one direction, resulting in perfect concentration. This is expressed in the New Testament in the statement that if the eye is single the whole body will be full of light, and in the *Bhagavad Gita* it is still more clearly and comprehensively given through the different chapters. In one it is beautifully put as the lighting up in us of the Supreme One, who then becomes visible. Let us meditate on that which is in us as the Highest Self, concentrate upon it, and will to work for it as dwelling in every human heart.

Irish Theosophist, July 1893

HIT THE MARK

Having taken the bow, the great weapon, let him place on it the arrow, sharpened by devotion. Then, having drawn it with a thought directed to that which is, hit the mark, O friend, — the Indestructible. OM is the bow, the Self is the arrow, Brahman is called its aim. It is to be hit by a man who is not thoughtless; and then as the arrow becomes one with the target, he will become one with Brahman. Know him alone as the Self, and leave off other words. He is the bridge of the Immortal. Meditate on the Self as OM. Hail to you that you may cross beyond the sea of darkness.

Mundaka Upanishad

Archery is a practice that symbolizes concentration. There is the archer, the arrow, the bow, and the target to be hit. To reach the mark it is necessary to concentrate the mind, the eye, and the body upon many points at once, while at the same time the string must be let go without disturbing the aim. The draw of the string with the arrow must be even and steady on the line of sight, and when grasp, draw, aim, and line are perfected, the arrow must be loosed smoothly at the moment of full draw, so that by the bow's recoil it may be carried straight to the mark. This is spiritual archery, and it is to this sort that the verse from the *Mundaka Upanishad* refers.

In archery among men a firm position must be assumed, and in the pursuit of truth this firm position must be taken up and not relaxed, if the object in view is to be ever attained. The eye must not wander from the target, for, if it does, the arrow will fly wide or fall short of its goal. So if we start out to reach the goal of wisdom, the mind and heart must not be permitted to wander, for the path is narrow and the wanderings of a day may cause us years of effort to find the road again.

The quality of the bow makes a great difference in the results attained by the archer. If it is not a good bow of strong texture and with a good spring to it, the missiles will not fly straight or with sufficient force to do the work required; and so with the man himself who is his own bow, if he has not the sort of nature that enables him to meet all the requirements, his work as a spiritual archer will fall that much short. But even as the bow made of wood or steel is subject to the alterations of state, so we are encouraged by the thought that the laws of karma and reincarnation show us that in other lives and new bodies we may do better work. The archer says too that the bow often seems to alter with the weather or other earthly changes, and will on some days do much better work than on others. The same thing is found by the observing theosophist, who comes to know that he too is subject from time to time to changes in his nature which enable him to accomplish more and to be nearer the spiritual condition. But the string of the bow must always be strung tight; and this, in spiritual archery, is the fixed determination to always strive for the goal.

When the arrow is aimed and loosed it must be slightly raised to allow for the trajectory, for if not it will fall short. This corresponds on its plane with one of the necessities of our human constitution, in that we must have a high mental and spiritual aim if we are to hit high. We cannot go quite as high as the aim, but have to thus allow for the trajectory that comes about from the limitations of our nature; the trajectory of the arrow is due to the force of gravity acting on it, and our aspirations have the same curve in consequence of the calls of the senses, hereditary defects, and wrong habits that never permit us to do as much as we would wish to do.

Let us hit the mark, O friend! and that mark is the indestructible, the highest spiritual life we are at any time capable of.

The Path, September 1890

RULES IN OCCULTISM

STUDENT.   Are there any rules, binding on all, in white magic or good occultism? I mean rules similar to the ten commandments of the Christians, or the rules for the protection of life, liberty, and property recognized by human law.

SAGE.   There are such rules of the most stringent character, the breaking of which is never wiped out save by expiation. Those rules are not made up by some brain or mind, but flow from the laws of nature, of mind, and of soul. Hence they are impossible of nullification. One may break them and seem to escape for a whole life or for more than a life; but the very breaking of them sets in motion at once other causes which begin to make effects, and most unerringly those effects at last react on the violator. Karma here acts as it does elsewhere, and becomes a Nemesis who, though sometimes slow, is fate itself in its certainty.

STUDENT.   It is not, then, the case that when an occultist violates a rule some other adept or agent starts out like a detective or policeman and brings the culprit to justice at a bar or tribunal such as we sometimes read of in the imaginative works of mystical writers or novelists?

SAGE.   No, there is no such pursuit. On the contrary, all the fellow-adepts or students are but too willing to aid the offender, not in escaping punishment, but in sincerely trying to set counteracting causes in motion for the good of all. For the sin of one reacts on the whole human family. If, however, the culprit does not wish to do the amount of counteracting good, he is merely left alone to the law of nature, which is in fact that of his own inner life from which there can be no escape. In Lytton's novel, *Zanoni,* you will notice the grave Master, Mejnour, trying to aid Zanoni, even at the time when the latter was falling slowly but surely into the meshes twisted by himself that ended in his destruction. Mejnour knew the law and so did Zanoni.

The latter was suffering from some former error which he had to work out; the former, if himself too stern and unkind, would later on come to the appropriate grief for such a mistake. But meanwhile he was bound to help his friend, as are all those who really believe in brotherhood.

STUDENT.   What one of those rules in any way corresponds to "Thou shalt not steal"?

SAGE.   That one which was long ago expressed by the ancient sage in the words, "Do not covet the wealth of any creature." This is better than "Thou shalt not steal," for you cannot steal unless you covet. If you steal for hunger you may be forgiven, but you coveted the food for a purpose, just as another covets merely for the sake of possession. The wealth of others includes all their possessions, and does not mean mere money alone. Their ideas, their private thoughts, their mental forces, powers, and faculties, their psychic powers — all, indeed, on all planes that they own or have. While they in that realm are willing to give it all away, it must not be coveted by another.

You have no right, therefore, to enter into the mind of another who has not given the permission and take from him what is not yours. You become a burglar on the mental and psychic plane when you break this rule. You are forbidden taking anything for personal gain, profit, advantage, or use. But you may take what is for general good, if you are far enough advanced and good enough to be able to extricate the personal element from it. This rule would, you can see, cut off all those who are well known to every observer, who want psychic powers for themselves and their own uses. If such persons had those powers of inner sight and hearing that they so much want, no power could prevent them from committing theft on the unseen planes wherever they met a nature that was not protected. And as most of us are very far from perfect, so far, indeed, that we must work for many lives, yet the Masters of Wisdom do not aid our defective natures in the getting of weapons that would cut our own hands. For the law acts implacably, and the breaches made would find their end and result in long after years. The Black Lodge, however, is very willing to let any poor, weak, or sinful mortal get such power, because that would swell the number of victims they so much require.

STUDENT.   Is there any rule corresponding to "Thou shalt not bear false witness"?

SAGE.   Yes; the one which requires you never to inject into the brain of another a false or untrue thought. As we can project our thoughts to another's mind, we must not throw untrue ones to another. It comes before him, and he, overcome by its strength perhaps, finds it echoing in him, and it is a false witness speaking falsely within, confusing and confounding the inner spectator who lives on thought.

STUDENT.   How can one prevent the natural action of the mind when pictures of the private lives of others rise before one?

SAGE.   That is difficult for the run of men. Hence the mass have not the power in general; it is kept back as much as possible. But when the trained soul looks about in the realm of soul it is also able to direct its sight, and when it finds rising up a picture of what it should not voluntarily take, it turns its face away. A warning comes with all such pictures which must be obeyed. This is not a rare rule or piece of information, for there are many natural clairvoyants who know it very well, though many of them do not think that others have the same knowledge.

STUDENT.   What do you mean by a warning coming with the picture?

SAGE.   In this realm the slightest thought becomes a voice or a picture. All thoughts make pictures. Every person has his private thoughts and desires. Around these he makes also a picture of his wish for privacy, and that to the clairvoyant becomes a voice or picture of warning which seems to say it must be let alone. With some it may assume the form of a person who says not to approach, with others it will be a voice, with still others a simple but certain knowledge that the matter is sacred. All these varieties depend on the psychological idiosyncrasies of the seer.

STUDENT.   What kind of thought or knowledge is expected from these rules?

SAGE.   General, and philosophical, religious, and moral. That is to say, there is no law of copyright or patent which is purely human in invention and belongs to the competitive system. When a man thinks out truly a philosophical problem it is not his under the laws of nature; it belongs to all; he is not in this realm entitled to any glory, to any profit, to any private use in it. Hence the seer may take as much of it as he pleases, but must on his part not claim it or use it for himself. Similarly with other generally beneficial matters. They are for all. If a Spencer thinks out a long series of wise things good for all men, the seer can take them all. Indeed, but few thinkers do any original thinking. They pride themselves on doing so, but in fact their seeking minds go out all over the world of mind and take from those of slower movement what is good and true, and then make them their own, sometimes gaining glory, sometimes money, and in this age claiming all as theirs and profiting by it.

The Path, January 1895

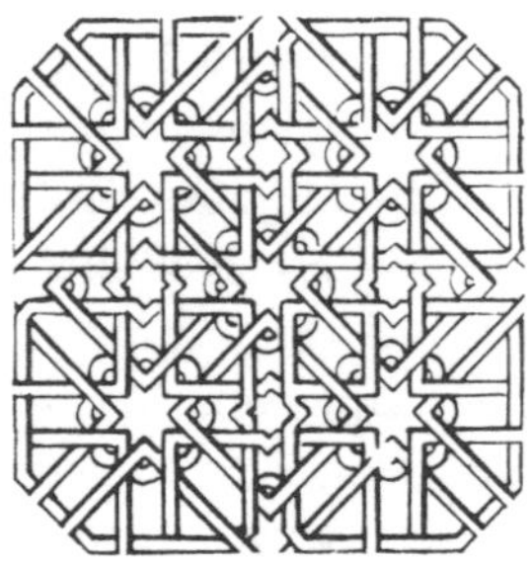

THE DWELLER OF THE THRESHOLD

Has such a being any existence? Has any one ever seen it? Are there many or several, and has it any sex?

Such are the questions asked by nearly all students who read theosophical books. Some of those who all their life believed in fairies in secret and in the old tales of giants, have proceeded to test the question by calling upon the horrid shade to appear and freeze their blood with the awful eyes that Bulwer Lytton has made so famous in his "Zanoni." But the Dweller is not to be wooed in such a way, and has not appeared at all, but by absolute silence leads the invoker to at last scout the idea altogether.

But this same inquirer then studies theosophical books with diligence, and enters after a time on the attempt to find out his own inner nature. All this while the Dweller has waited, and, indeed, we may say, in complete ignorance as yet of the neophyte's existence. When the study has proceeded far enough to wake up long dormant senses and tendencies, the Dweller begins to feel that such a person as this student is at work. Certain influences are then felt, but not always with clearness, and at first never ascribed to the agency of what had long ago been relegated to the lumber-room of exploded superstitions. The study goes still farther and yet farther, until the awful Thing has revealed itself; and when that happens, it is not a superstition nor is it disbelieved. It can then never be gotten rid of, but will stay as a constant menace until it is triumphed over *and left behind.*

When Glyndon was left by Mejnour in the old castle in Italy, he found two vases which he had received directions not to open. But disobeying these he took out the stoppers, and at once the room was filled with intoxication, and soon the awful, loathsome creature appeared whose blazing eyes shone with malignant glare and penetrated to Glyndon's soul with a rush of horror such as he had never known.

In this story Lytton desired to show that the opening of the vases is like the approach of an enquirer to the secret recesses of his own nature. He opens the receptacles, and at first is full of joy and a sort of intoxication due to the new solutions offered for every problem in life and to the dimly seen vistas of power and advancement that open before him. If the vases *are kept open long enough*, the Dweller of the Threshold surely appears, and no man is exempt from the sight. Goodness is not sufficient to prevent its appearance, because even the good man who finds a muddy place in the way to his destination must of necessity pass through it to reach the end.

We must ask next, WHAT is the Dweller? It is the combined evil influence that is the result of the wicked thoughts and acts of the age in which any one may live, and it assumes to each student a definite shape at each appearance, being always either of one sort or changing each time. So that with one it may be as Bulwer Lytton pictured it, or with another only a dread horror, or even of any other sort of shape. It is specialized for each student and given its form by the tendencies and natural physical and psychical combinations that belong to his family and nation.

Where, then, does it dwell? is the very natural inquiry which will follow. It dwells in its own plane, and that may be understood in this manner.

Around each person are planes or zones, beginning with spirit and running down to gross matter. These zones extend, within their lateral boundaries, all around the being. That is to say, if we figure ourselves as being in the centre of a sphere, we will find that there is no way of escaping or skipping any one zone, because it extends in every direction until we pass its lateral boundary.

When the student has at last gotten hold of a real aspiration and some glimmer of the blazing goal of truth where Masters stand, and has also aroused the determination to know and to be, the whole bent of his nature, day and night, is to reach out beyond the limitations that hitherto had fettered his soul. No sooner does he begin thus to step a little forward, than he reaches the zone just beyond mere bodily and mental sensations. At first the minor dwellers of the threshold are aroused, and they in temptation, in bewilderment, in doubt or confusion, assail him. He only feels the effect, for they do not reveal themselves as shapes. But persistence in the work takes the inner man farther along, and with that progress comes a realization to the outer mind of the experiences met, until at last he has waked up the whole force of the evil power that naturally is arrayed against the good end he has set before him. Then the Dweller takes what form it may. That it does take some definite shape or impress itself with palpable horror is a fact testified to by many students.

One of those related to me that he saw it as an enormous slug with evil eyes whose malignancy could not be described. As he retreated — that is, grew fearful — , it seemed joyful and portentous, and when retreat was complete it was not. Then he fell further back in thought and action, having occasionally moments of determination to retrieve his lost ground. Whenever these came to him, the dreadful slug again appeared, only to leave him when he had given up again his aspirations. And he knew that he was only making the fight, if ever he should take it up again, all the harder.

Another says that he has seen the Dweller concentrated in the apparent form of a dark and sinister-looking man, whose slightest motions, whose merest glance, expressed the intention and ability to destroy the student's reason, and only the strongest effort of will and faith could dispel the evil influence. And the same student at other times has felt it as a vague, yet terrible, horror that seemed to enwrap him in its folds. Before this he has retreated for the time to prepare himself by strong self-study to be pure and brave for the next attack.

These things are not the same as the temptations of Saint Anthony. In his case he seems to have induced an hysterical erotic condition, in which the unvanquished secret thoughts of his own heart found visible appearance.

The Dweller of the Threshold is not the product of the brain, but is an influence found in a plane that is extraneous to the student, but in which his success or failure will be due to his own purity. It is not a thing to be dreaded by mere dilettanti theosophists; and no earnest one who feels himself absolutely called to work persistently to the highest planes of development for the good of humanity, and not for his own, need fear aught that heaven or hell holds.

The Path, December 1888   EUSEBIO URBAN

'FORMS' OF ELEMENTALS

STUDENT.   What principal idea would it be well for me to dwell upon in my studies on the subject of elementals?

SAGE.   You ought to clearly fix in your mind and fully comprehend a few facts and the laws relating to them. As the elemental world is wholly different from the one visible to you, the laws governing them and their actions cannot as yet be completely defined in terms now used either by scientific or metaphysical schools. For that reason, only a partial description is possible. Some of those facts I will give you, it being well understood that I am not including all classes of elemental beings in my remarks.

First, then, Elementals have no form.

STUDENT.   You mean, I suppose, that they have no limited form or body as ours, having a surface upon which sensation appears to be located.

SAGE.   Not only so, but also that they have not even a shadowy, vague, astral form such as is commonly ascribed to ghosts. They have no distinct personal form in which to reveal themselves.

STUDENT.   How am I to understand that, in view of the instances given by Bulwer Lytton and others of appearances of elementals in certain forms?

SAGE.   The shape given to or assumed by any elemental is always subjective in its origin. It is produced by the person who sees, and who, in order to be more sensible of the elemental's presence, has unconsciously given it a form. Or it may be due to a collective impression on many individuals, resulting in the assumption of a definite shape which is the result of the combined impressions.

STUDENT.   Is this how we may accept as true the story of

Luther's seeing the devil?

SAGE.   Yes. Luther from his youth had imagined a personal devil, the head of the fraternity of wicked ones, who had a certain specific form. This instantly clothed the elementals that Luther evoked, either through intense enthusiasm or from disease, with the old image reared and solidified in his mind; and he called it the Devil.

STUDENT.   That reminds me of a friend who told me that in his youth he saw the conventional devil walk out of the fire place and pass across the room, and that ever since he believed the devil had an objective existence.

SAGE.   In the same way also you can understand the extraordinary occurrences at Salem in the United States, when hysterical and mediumistic women and children saw the devil and also various imps of different shapes. Some of these gave the victims information. They were all elementals, and took their illusionary forms from the imaginations and memory of the poor people who were afflicted.

STUDENT.   But there are cases where a certain form always appears. Such as a small, curiously-dressed woman who had never existed in the imagination of those seeing her; and other regularly recurring appearances. How were those produced, since the persons never had such a picture before them?

SAGE.   These pictures are found in the aura of the person, and are due to pre-natal impressions. Each child emerges into life the possessor of pictures floating about and clinging to it, derived from the mother; and thus you can go back an enormous distance in time for these pictures, all through the long line of your descent. It is a part of the action of the same law which causes effects upon a child's body through influences acting on the mother during gestation.*

* See *Isis Unveiled* in the chapter on Teratology.

STUDENT.   In order, then, to know the cause of any such appearance, one must be able to look back, not only into the person's present life, but also into the ancestor's past?

SAGE.   Precisely. And for that reason an occultist is not hasty in giving his opinion on these particular facts. He can only state the general law, for a life might be wasted in needless investigation of an unimportant past. You can see that there would be no justification for going over a whole lifetime's small affairs in order to tell a person at what time or juncture an image was projected before his mind. Thousands of such impressions are made every year. That they are not *developed into memory* does not prove their non-existence. Like the unseen picture upon the photographer's sensitive plate, they lie awaiting the hour of development.

STUDENT.   In what way should I figure to myself the essence of an elemental and its real mode of existence?

SAGE.   You should think of them as *centres of energy* only, that act always in accordance with the laws of the plane of nature to which they belong.

STUDENT.   Is it not just as if we were to say that gunpowder is an elemental and will invariably explode when lighted? That is, that the elementals know no rules of either wrong or right, but surely act when the incitement to their natural action is present? They are thus, I suppose, said to be implacable.

SAGE.   Yes; they are like the lightning which flashes or destroys as the varying circumstances compel. It has no regard for man, or love, or beauty, or goodness, but may as quickly kill the innocent, or burn the property of the good as of the wicked man.

STUDENT.   What next?

SAGE.   That the elementals live in and through all objects, as well as beyond the earth's atmosphere.

STUDENT. Do you mean that a certain class of elementals, for instance, exist in this mountain, and float unobstructed through men, earth, rocks, and trees?

SAGE. Yes, and not only that, but at the same time, penetrating that class of elementals, there may be another class which float not only through rocks, trees, and men, but also through the first of the classes referred to.

STUDENT. Do they perceive these objects obstructive for us, through which they thus float?

SAGE. No, generally they do not. In exceptional cases they do, and even then never with the same sort of cognition that we have. For them the objects have no existence. A large block of stone or iron offers for them no limits or density. It may, however, make an impression on them by way of change of color or sound, but not by way of density or obstruction.

STUDENT. Is it not something like this, that a current of electricity passes through a hard piece of copper wire, while it will not pass through an unresisting space of air.

SAGE. That serves to show that the thing which is dense to one form of energy may be open to another. Continuing your illustration, we see that man can pass through air but is stopped by metal. So that "hardness" for us is not "hardness" for electricity. Similarly, that which may stop an elemental is not a body that we call hard, but something which for us is intangible and invisible, but presents to them an adamantine front.

STUDENT. I thank you for your instruction.

SAGE. Strive to deserve further enlightenment!

The Path, October 1888

ASTRAL INTOXICATION

There is such a thing as being intoxicated in the course of an unwise pursuit of what we erroneously imagine is spirituality. In the Christian Bible it is very wisely directed to "prove all" and to hold only to that which is good; this advice is just as important to the student of occultism who thinks that he has separated himself from those "inferior" people engaged either in following a dogma or in tipping tables for messages from deceased relatives — or enemies — as it is to spiritists who believe in the "summerland" and "returning spirits."

The placid surface of the sea of spirit is the only mirror in which can be caught undisturbed the reflections of spiritual things. When a student starts upon the path and begins to see spots of light flash out now and then, or balls of golden fire roll past him, it does not mean that he is beginning to see the real Self — pure spirit. A moment of deepest peace or wonderful revealings given to the student, is *not* the awful moment when one is about to see his spiritual guide, much less his own soul. Nor are psychical splashes of blue flame, nor visions of things that afterwards come to pass, nor sights of small sections of the astral light with its wonderful photographs of past or future, nor the sudden ringing of distant fairy-like bells, any proof that you are cultivating spirituality. These things, and still more curious things, will occur when you have passed a little distance on the way, but they are only the mere outposts of a new land which is itself wholly material, and only one remove from the plane of gross physical consciousness.

The liability to be carried off and intoxicated by these phenomena is to be guarded against. We should watch, note and discriminate in all these cases; place them down for future reference, to be related to some law, or for comparison with other circumstances of a like sort. The power that Nature has of deluding us is endless, and if we stop at these matters she will let us go no further. It is not that any person or power in nature has declared that if we do so and so we must stop, but when one is carried off by what Boehme calls "God's wonders," the result is an intoxication that produces confusion of the intellect. Were one, for instance, to regard every picture seen in the astral light as a spiritual experience, he might truly after a while brook no contradiction upon the subject, but that would be merely because he was drunk with this kind of wine. While he proceeded with his indulgence and neglected his true progress, which is always dependent upon his purity of motive and conquest of his known or ascertainable defects, nature went on accumulating the store of illusory appearances with which he satiated himself.

It is certain that any student who devotes himself to these astral happenings will see them increase. But were our whole life devoted to and rewarded by an enormous succession of phenomena, it is also equally certain that the casting off of the body would be the end of all that sort of experience, without our having added really anything to our stock of true knowledge.

The astral plane, which is the same as that of our psychic senses, is as full of strange sights and sounds as an untrodden South American forest, and has to be well understood before the student can stay there long without danger. While we can overcome the dangers of a forest by the use of human inventions, whose entire object is the physical destruction of the noxious things encountered there, we have no such aids when treading the astral labyrinth. We may be physically brave and say that no fear can enter into us, but no untrained or merely curious seeker is able to say just what effect will result to his outer senses from the attack or influence encountered by the psychical senses.

And the person who revolves selfishly around himself as a center is in greater danger of delusion than any one else, for he has not the assistance that comes from being united in thought with all other sincere seekers. One may stand in a dark house where none of the objects can be distinguished and quite plainly see all that is illuminated outside; in the same way we can see from out of the blackness of our own house — our hearts — the objects now and then illuminated outside by the astral light; but we gain nothing. We must first dispel the *inner* darkness before trying to see into the darkness without; we must *know ourselves* before knowing things extraneous to ourselves.

This is not the road that seems easiest to students. Most of them find it far pleasanter and, as they think, faster work, to look on all these outside allurements, and to cultivate all psychic senses, to the exclusion of real spiritual work.

The true road is plain and easy to find, it is so easy that very many would-be students miss it because they cannot believe it to be so simple.

'The way lies through the heart';
Ask there and wander not;
Knock loud, nor hesitate
Because at first the sounds
Reverberating, seem to mock thee.
Nor, when the door swings wide,
Revealing shadows black as night,
Must thou recoil.
Within, the Master's messengers
Have waited patiently:
That Master is Thyself!

The Path, October 1887

MENTAL DISCIPLINE

STUDENT. Is there not some attitude of mind which one should in truth assume in order to understand the occult in Nature?

SAGE. Such attitude of mind must be attained as will enable one to look into the realities of things. The mind must escape from the mere formalities and conventions of life, even though outwardly one seems to obey all of them, and should be firmly established on the truth that Man is a copy of the Universe and has in himself a portion of the Supreme Being. To the extent this is realized will be the clearness of perception of truth. A realization of this leads inevitably to the conclusion that all other men and beings are united with us, and this removes the egotism which is the result of the notion of separateness. When the truth of Unity is understood, then distinctions due to comparisons made like the Pharisee's, that one is better than his neighbor, disappear from the mind, leaving it more pure and free to act.

STUDENT. What would you point out as a principal foe to the mind's grasping of truth?

SAGE. The principal foe of a secondary nature is what was once called *phantasy*; that is, the reappearance of thoughts and images due to recollection or memory. Memory is an important power, but mind in itself is not memory. Mind is restless and wandering in its nature, and must be controlled. Its wandering disposition is necessary or stagnation would result. But it can be controlled and fixed upon an object or idea. Now as we are constantly looking at and hearing of new things, the natural restlessness of the mind becomes prominent when we set about pinning it down. Then memory of many objects, things, subjects, duties, persons, circumstances, and affairs brings up before it the various pictures and thoughts belonging to them. After these the mind at once tries to go, and we find ourselves wandering from the point. It must hence follow that the storing of a multiplicity of useless and surely-recurring thoughts is an obstacle to the acquirement of truth. And this obstacle is the very one peculiar to our present style of life.

STUDENT.   Can you mention some of the relations in which the sun stands to us and nature in respect to Occultism?

SAGE.   It has many such, and all important. But I would draw your attention first to the greater and more comprehensive. The sun is the center of our solar system. The life-energies of that system come to it through the sun, which is a focus or reflector for the spot in space where the real center is. And not only comes mere life through that focus, but also much more that is spiritual in its essence. The sun should therefore not only be looked at with the eye but thought of by the mind. It represents to the world what the Higher Self is to the man. It is the soul-center of the world with its six companions, as the Higher Self is the center for the six principles of man. So it supplies to those six principles of the man many spiritual essences and powers. He should for that reason think of it and not confine himself to gazing at it. So far as it acts materially in light, heat, and gravity, it will go on of itself, but man as a free agent must think upon it in order to gain what benefit can come only from his voluntary action in thought.

STUDENT.   Will you refer to some minor one?

SAGE.   Well, we sit in the sun for heat and possible chemical effects. But if at the same time that we do this we also think on it as the sun in the sky and of its possible essential nature, we thereby draw from it some of its energy not otherwise touched. This can also be done on a dark day when clouds obscure the sky, and some of the benefit thus be obtained. Natural mystics, learned and ignorant, have discovered this for themselves here and there, and have often adopted the practice. But it depends, as you see, upon the mind.

STUDENT.   Does the mind actually do anything when it takes up a thought and seeks for more light?

SAGE.   It actually does. A thread, or a finger, or a long darting current flies out from the brain to seek for knowledge. It goes in all directions and touches all other minds it can reach so as to receive the information if possible. This is telepathically, so to say, accomplished. There are no patents on true knowledge of philosophy nor copyrights in the realm. Personal rights of personal life are fully respected, save by potential black magicians who would take anyone's property. But general truth belongs to all, and when the unseen messenger from one mind arrives and touches the real mind of another, that other gives up to it what it may have of truth about general subjects. So the mind's finger or wire flies until it gets the thought or seed-thought from the other and makes it its own. But our modern competitive system and selfish desire for gain and fame is constantly building a wall around people's minds to everyone's detriment.

STUDENT.   Do you mean that the action you describe is natural, usual, and universal, or only done by those who know how and are conscious of it?

SAGE.   It is universal and whether the person is aware or not of what is going on. Very few are able to perceive it in themselves, but that makes no difference. It is done always. When you sit down to earnestly think on a philosophical or ethical matter, for instance, your mind flies off, touching other minds, and from them you get varieties of thought. If you are not well-balanced and psychically purified, you will often get thoughts that are not correct. Such is your Karma and the Karma of the race. But if you are sincere and try to base yourself on right philosophy, your mind will naturally reject wrong notions. You can see in this how it is that systems of thought are made and kept going, even though foolish, incorrect, or pernicious.

STUDENT.   What mental attitude and aspiration are the best safeguards in this, as likely to aid the mind in these searches to reject error and not let it fly into the brain?

SAGE.   Unselfishness, Altruism in theory and practice, desire to do the will of the Higher Self which is the "Father in Heaven," devotion to the human race. Subsidiary to these are discipline, correct thinking, and good education.

STUDENT.   Is the uneducated man, then, in a worse condition?

SAGE.   Not necessarily so. The very learned are so immersed in one system that they reject nearly all thoughts not in accord with preconceived notions. The sincere ignorant one is often able to get the truth but not able to express it. The ignorant masses generally hold in their minds the general truths of Nature, but are limited as to expression. And most of the best discoveries of scientific men have been obtained in this sub-conscious telepathic mode. Indeed, they often arrive in the learned brain from some obscure and so-called ignorant person, and then the scientific discoverer makes himself famous because of his power of expression and means for giving it out.

STUDENT.   Does this bear at all upon the work of the Adepts of all good Lodges?

SAGE.   It does. They have all the truths that could be desired, but at the same time are able to guard them from the seeking minds of those who are not yet ready to use them properly. But they often find the hour ripe and a scientific man ready, and then touch his cogitating mind with a picture of what he seeks. He then has a "flash" of thought in the line of his deliberations, as many of them have admitted. He gives it out to the world, becomes famous, and the world wiser. This is constantly done by the Adepts, but now and then they give out larger expositions of Nature's truths, as in the case of H.P.B. This is not at first generally accepted, as personal gain and fame are not advanced by any admission of benefit from the writings of another, but as it is done with a purpose, for the use of a succeeding century, it will do its work at the proper time.

STUDENT.   How about the Adepts knowing what is going on in the world of thought, in the West, for instance?

SAGE.   They have only to voluntarily and consciously connect their minds with those of the dominant thinkers of the day to at once discover what has been or is being worked out in thought and to review it all. This they constantly do, and as constantly incite to further elaborations or changes by throwing out the suggestion in the mental plane so that seeking and receptive minds may use it.

The Path, December 1894

MANTRAMS

STUDENT. You spoke of mantrams by which we could control elementals on guard over hidden treasure. What is a mantram?

SAGE. A mantram is a collection of words which, when sounded in speech, induce certain vibrations not only in the air, but also in the finer ether, thereby producing certain effects.

STUDENT. Are the words taken at haphazard?

SAGE. Only by those who, knowing nothing of mantrams, yet use them.

STUDENT. May they, then, be used according to rule and also irregularly? Can it be possible that people who know absolutely nothing of their existence or field of operations should at the same time make use of them? Or is it something like digestion, of which so many people know nothing whatever, while they in fact are dependent upon its proper use for their existence? I crave your indulgence because I know nothing of the subject.

SAGE. The "common people" in almost every country make use of them continually, but even in that case the principle at the bottom is the same as in the other. In a new country where folk-lore has not yet had time to spring up, the people do not have as many as in such a land as India or in long settled parts of Europe. The aborigines, however, in any country will be possessed of them.

STUDENT. You do not now infer that they are used by Europeans for the controlling of elementals?

SAGE. No. I refer to their effect in ordinary intercourse between human beings. And yet there are many men in Europe, as well as in Asia, who can thus control animals, but those are nearly always special cases. There are men in Germany, Austria, Italy, and Ireland who can bring about extraordinary effects on horses, cattle, and the like, by peculiar sounds uttered in a certain way. In those instances the sound used is a mantram of only one member, and will act only on the particular animal that the user knows it can rule.

STUDENT.   Do these men know the rules governing the matter? Are they able to convey it to another?

SAGE.   Generally not. It is a gift self-found or inherited, and they only know that it can be done by them, just as a mesmerizer knows he can do a certain thing with a wave of his hand, but is totally ignorant of the principle. They are as ignorant of the base of this strange effect as your modern physiologists are of the function and cause of such a common thing as yawning.

STUDENT.   Under what head should we put this unconscious exercise of power?

SAGE.   Under the head of natural magic, that materialistic science can never crush out. It is a touch with nature and her laws always preserved by the masses, who, while they form the majority of the population, are yet ignored by the "cultured classes." And so it will be discovered by you that it is not in London or Paris or New York drawing-rooms that you will find mantrams, whether regular or irregular, used by the people. "Society," too cultured to be natural, has adopted methods of speech intended to conceal and to deceive, so that natural mantrams can not be studied within its borders.

Single, natural mantrams are such words as "wife." When it is spoken it brings up in the mind all that is implied by the word. And if in another language, the word would be that corresponding to the same basic idea. And so with expressions of greater length, such as many slang sentences; thus, "I want to see the color of his money." There are also sentences applicable to certain individuals, the use of which involves a knowledge of the character of those to whom we speak. When these are used, a peculiar and lasting vibration is set up in the mind of the person affected, leading to a realization in action of the idea involved, or to a total change of life due to the appositeness of the subjects brought up and to the peculiar mental antithesis induced in the hearer. As soon as the effect begins to appear the mantram may be forgotten, since the *law of habit* then has sway in the brain.

Again, bodies of men are acted on by expressions having the mantramic quality; this is observed in great social or other disturbances. The reason is the same as before. A dominant idea is aroused that touches upon a want of the people or on an abuse which oppresses them, and the change and interchange in their brains between the idea and the form of words go on until the result is accomplished. To the occultist of powerful sight this is seen to be a "ringing" of the words coupled with the whole chain of feelings, interests, aspirations, and so forth, that grows faster and deeper as the time for the relief or change draws near. And the greater number of persons affected by the idea involved, the larger, deeper, and wider the result. A mild illustration may be found in Lord Beaconsfield of England. He knew about mantrams, and continually invented phrases of that quality. "Peace with honor" was one; "a scientific frontier" was another; and his last, intended to have a wider reach, but which death prevented his supplementing, was "Empress of India." King Henry of England also tried it without himself knowing why, when he added to his titles, "Defender of the Faith." With these hints numerous illustrations will occur to you.

STUDENT.   These mantrams have only to do with human beings as between each other. They do not affect elementals, as I judge from what you say. And they are not dependent upon the *sound* so much as upon words bringing up ideas. Am I right in this; and is it the case that there is a field in which certain vocalizations produce effects in the *Akasa* by means of which men, animals, and elementals alike can be influenced, without regard to their knowledge of any known language?

SAGE.   You are right. We have only spoken of natural, unconsciously-used mantrams. The scientific mantrams belong to the class you last referred to. It is to be doubted whether

50

they can be found in modern Western languages — especially among English speaking people who are continually changing and adding to their spoken words to such an extent that the English of today could hardly be understood by Chaucer's predecessors. It is in the ancient Sanscrit and the language which preceded it that mantrams are hidden. The laws governing their use are also to be found in those languages, and not in any modern philological store.

STUDENT.   Suppose, though, that one acquires a knowledge of ancient and correct mantrams, could he affect a person speaking English, and by the use of English words?

SAGE.   He could; and all adepts have the power to translate a strictly regular mantram into any form of language, so that a single sentence thus uttered by them will have an immense effect on the person addressed, whether it be by letter or word of mouth.

STUDENT.   Is there no way in which we might, as it were, imitate those adepts in this?

SAGE.   Yes, you should study simple forms of mantramic quality, for the purpose of thus reaching the hidden mind of all the people who need spiritual help. You will find now and then some expression that has resounded in the brain, at last producing such a result that he who heard it turns his mind to spiritual things.

STUDENT.   I thank you for your instruction.

SAGE.   May the Brahmamantram guide you to the everlasting truth — OM.

The Path, August 1888

UNIVERSAL APPLICATIONS
OF DOCTRINE

During the last few years in which so much writing has been done in the theosophical field of effort, a failure to make broad or universal applications of the doctrines brought forward can be noticed. With the exception of H.P. Blavatsky, our writers have confined themselves to narrow views, chiefly as to the state of man after death or how Karma affects him in life. As to the latter law, the greatest consideration has been devoted to deciding how it modifies our pleasure or our pain, and then as to whether in Devachan there will be compensation for failures of Karma; while others write upon reincarnation as if only mankind were subject to that law. And the same limited treatment is adopted in treating of or practising many other theories and doctrines of the Wisdom Religion. After fourteen years of activity it is now time that the members of our society should make universal the application of each and every admitted doctrine or precept, and not confine them to their own selfish selves.

In order to make my meaning clear I purpose in this paper to attempt an outline of how such universal applications of some of our doctrines should be made.

Before taking up any of these I would draw the attention of those who believe in the *Upanishads* to the constant insistence throughout those sacred books upon the identity of man with Brahma, or God, or nature, and to the universal application of all doctrines or laws.

In *Brihadaranyaka Upanishad** it is said:

> Tell me the Brahman which is visible, not invisible, the *atman* who is within all?
>
> This, thy Self who is within all. . . . He who breathes in the up-breathing, he is thy Self and within all. He who breathes in the down-breathing, he is thy Self and within all. He who breathes in the on-breathing, he is thy Self and within all. This is thy Self who is within all.

---

* 111 Adh., 4th Brah.

The 6th Brahmana is devoted to showing that all the worlds are woven in and within each other; and in the 7th the teacher declares that "the puller" or mover in all things whatsoever is the same Self which is in each man.

The questioners then proceed and draw forth the statement that "what is above the heavens, beneath the earth, embracing heaven and earth, past, present, and future, that is woven, like warp and woof, in the ether," and that the ether is "woven like warp and woof in the Imperishable." If this be so, then any law that affects man must govern every portion of the universe in which he lives.

And we find these sturdy men of old applying their doctrines in every direction. They use the laws of analogy and correspondences to solve deep questions. Why need we be behind them? If the entire great Self dwells in man, the body in all its parts must symbolize the greater world about. So we discover that space having sound as its distinguishing characteristic is figured in the human frame by the ear, as fire is by the eye, and, again, the eye showing forth the soul, for the soul alone conquers death, and that which in the *Upanishads* conquers death is fire.

It is possible in this manner to proceed steadily toward the acquirement of a knowledge of the laws of nature, not only those that are recondite, but also the more easily perceived. If we grant that the human body and organs are a figure, in little, of the universe, then let us ask the question, "By what is the astral light symbolized?" By the eye, and specially by the retina and its mode of action. On the astral light are received the pictures of all events and things, and on the retina are received the images of objects passing before the man. We find that these images on the retina remain for a specific period, capable of measurement, going through certain changes before fading completely away. Let us extend the result of this observation to the astral light, and we assume that it also goes through similar changes in respect to the pictures. From this it follows that the mass or totality of pictures made during any cycle must, in this great retina, have a period at the end of which they will have faded away. Such we find is the law as stated by those who know the Secret Doctrine. In order to arrive at the figures with which to represent this period, we have to calculate the proportion thus: as the time of fading from the human retina is to the healthy man's actual due of life, so is the time of fading from the astral light. The missing term may be discovered by working upon the doctrine of the four yugas or ages and the length of one life of Brahma.

Now these theosophical doctrines which we have been at such pains to elaborate during all the years of our history are either capable of universal application or they are not. If they are not, then they are hardly worth the trouble we have bestowed upon them; and it would then have been much better for us had we devoted ourselves to some special departments of science.

But the great allurement that theosophy holds for those who follow it is that its doctrines are universal, solving all questions and applying to every department of nature so far as we know it. And advanced students declare that the same universal application prevails in regions far beyond the grasp of present science or of the average man's mind. So that, if a supposed law or application is formulated to us, either by ourselves or by some other person, we are at once able to prove it; for unless it can be applied in every direction — by correspondence, or is found to be one of the phases of some previously-admitted doctrine, we know that it is false doctrine or inaccurately stated. Thus all our doctrines can be proved and checked at every step. It is not necessary for us to have constant communications with the Adepts in order to make sure of our ground; all that we have to do is to see if any position we assume agrees with well-known principles already formulated and understood.

Bearing this in mind, we can confidently proceed to examine the great ideas in which so many of us believe, with a view of seeing how they may be applied in every direction. For if, instead of selfishly considering these laws in their effect upon our miserable selves, we ask how they apply everywhere, a means is furnished for the broadening of our horizon and the elimination of selfishness. And when also we apply the doctrines to all our acts and to all parts of the human being, we may begin to wake ourselves up to the real task set before us.

Let us look at Karma. It must be applied not only to the man but also to the Cosmos, to the globe upon which he lives. You know that, for the want of an English word, the period of one great day of evolution is called a Manwantara, or the reign of one Manu. These eternally succeed each other. In other words, each one of us is a unit, or a cell, if you please, in the great body or being of Manu, and just as we see ourselves making Karma and reincarnating for the purpose of carrying off Karma, so the great being Manu dies at the end of a Manwantara, and after the period of rest reincarnates once more, the sum total of all that we have made him — or it. And when I say "we," I mean all the beings on whatever plane or planet who are included in that Manwantara. Therefore this Manwantara is just exactly what the last Manwantara made it, and so the next Manwantara after this — millions of years off — will be the sum or result of this one, plus all that have preceded it.

How much have you thought upon the effect of Karma upon the animals, the plants, the minerals, the elemental beings? Have you been so selfish as to suppose that they are not affected by you? Is it true that man himself has no responsibility upon him for the vast numbers of ferocious and noxious animals, for the deadly serpents and scorpions, the devastating lions and tigers, that make a howling wilderness of some corners of the earth and terrorize the people of India and elsewhere? It cannot be true. But as the Apostle of the Christians said, it is true that the whole of creation waits upon man and groans that he keeps back the enlightenment of all. What happens when, with intention, you crush out the life of a common croton bug? Well, it is destroyed and you forget it. But you brought it to an untimely end, short though its life would have been. Imagine this being done at hundreds of thousands of places in the State. Each of these little creatures had life and energy; each some degree of intelligence. The sum total of the effects of all these deaths of small things must be appreciable. If not, then our doctrines are wrong and there is no wrong in putting out the life of a human being.

Let us go a little higher, to the bird kingdom and that of four-footed beasts. Every day in the shooting season in England vast quantities of birds are killed for sport, and in other places such intelligent and inoffensive animals as deer. These have a higher intelligence than insects, a wider scope of feeling. Is there no effect under Karma for all these deaths? And what is the difference between wantonly killing a deer and murdering an idiot? Very little to my mind. Why is it, then, that even delicate ladies will enjoy the recital of a bird or deer hunt? It is their

Karma that they are the descendants of long generations of Europeans who some centuries ago, with the aid of the church, decided that animals had no souls and therefore could be wantonly slaughtered. The same Karma permits the grandson of the Queen of England who calls herself the defender of the faith — of Jesus — to have great preparations made for his forth-coming visit to India to the end that he shall enjoy several weeks of tiger-hunting, pig-sticking, and the destruction of any and every bird that may fly in his way.

We therefore find ourselves ground down by the Karma of our national stem, so that we are really almost unable to tell what thoughts are the counterfeit presentments of the thoughts of our forefathers, and what self-born in our own minds.

Let us now look at Reincarnation, Devachan, and Karma.

It has been the custom of theosophists to think upon these subjects in respect only to the whole man — that is to say, respecting the ego.

But what of its hourly and daily application? If we believe in the doctrine of the One Life, then every cell in these material bodies must be governed by the same laws. Each cell must be *a life* and have its karma, devachan, and reincarnation. Every one of these cells upon incarnating among the others in our frame must be affected by the character of those it meets; and we make that character. Every thought upon reaching its period dies. It is soon reborn, and coming back from its devachan it finds either bad or good companions provided for it. Therefore every hour of life is fraught with danger or with help. How can it be possible that a few hours a week devoted to theosophic thought and action can counteract — even in the gross material cells — the effect of nearly a whole week spent in indifference, frivolity, or selfishness? This mass of poor or bad thought will form a resistless tide that shall sweep away all your good resolves at the first opportunity.

This will explain why devoted students often fail. They have waited for a particular hour or day to try their strength, and when the hour came they had none. If it was anger they had resolved to conquer, instead of trying to conquer it at an offered opportunity they ran away from the chance so as to escape the trial; or they did not meet the hourly small trials that would, if successfully passed, have given them a great reserve of strength, so that no time of greater trial would have been able to overcome them.

Now as to the theory of the evolution of the macrocosm in its application to the microcosm, man.

The hermetic philosophy held that man is a copy of the greater universe; that he is a little universe in himself, governed by the same laws as the great one, and in the small proportions of a human being showing all those greater laws in operation, only reduced in time or sweep. This is the rule to which H.P. Blavatsky adheres, and which is found running through all the ancient mysteries and initiations.

It is said that our universe is a collection of atoms or molecules — called also *"lives"*; living together and through each the spirit struggles to reach consciousness, and that this struggle is governed by a law compelling it to go on in or between periods. In any period of such struggle some of these atoms or collections of molecules are left over, as it were, to renew the battle in the next period, and hence the state of the universe at any time of manifestation — or the state of each newly-manifested universe — must be the result of what was done in the preceding period.

Coming down to the man, we find that he is a collection of molecules or *lives* or cells, each striving with the other, and all affected for either good or bad results by the spiritual aspirations or want of them in the man who is the guide or god, so to say, of his little universe. When he is born, the molecules or cells or lives that are to compose his physical and astral forms are from that moment under his reign, and during the period of his smaller life they pass through a small manvantara just as the lives in the universe do, and when he dies he leaves them all impressed with the force and color of his thoughts and aspirations, ready to be used in composing the houses of other egos.

Now here is a great responsibility revealed to us of a double character.

The first is for effects produced on and left in what we call matter in the molecules, when they come to be used by other egos, for they must act upon the latter for benefit or the reverse.

The second is for the effect on the molecules themselves in this, that there are lives or entities in all — or rather they are all lives — who are either aided or retarded in their evolution by reason of the proper or improper use man made of this matter that was placed in his charge.

Without stopping to argue about what matter is, it will be sufficient to state that it is held to be co-eternal with what is called "spirit." That is, as it is put in the *Bhagavad-Gita*: "He who is spirit is also matter." Or, in other words, spirit is the opposite pole to matter of the Absolute. But of course this matter we speak of is not what we see about us, for the latter is only in fact phenomena of matter: even science holds that we do not really see matter.

Now during a manvantara or period of manifestation, the egos incarnating must use over and over again in any world upon which they are incarnating the matter that belongs to it.

So, therefore, we are now using in our incarnations matter that has been used by ourselves and other egos over and over again, and are affected by the various tendencies impressed in it. And, similarly, we are leaving behind us for future races that which will help or embarrass them in their future lives.

This is a highly important matter, whether reincarnation be a true doctrine or not. For if each new nation is only a mass of new egos or souls, it must be much affected by the matter-environment left behind by nations and races that have disappeared forever.

But for us who believe in reincarnation it has additional force, showing us one strong reason why universal brotherhood should be believed in and practised.

The other branch of the responsibility is just as serious. The doctrine that removes death from the universe and declares that all is composed of innumerable lives, constantly changing places with each other, contains in it of necessity the theory that man himself is full of these lives and that all are traveling up the long road of evolution.

The secret doctrine holds that we are full of kingdoms of entities who depend upon us, so to say, for salvation.

How enormous, then, is this responsibility, that we not only are to be judged for what we do with ourselves as a whole, but also for what we do for those unseen beings who are dependent upon us for light.

The Path, October 1889

MECHANICAL THEOSOPHY

The earnest, devoted student can hardly believe that there exist any theosophists sincerely holding a belief in theosophical doctrines but who are, at the same time, found to have such a mechanical conception of them as permits one to retain undisturbed many old dogmas which are diametrically opposed to Theosophy. Yet we have such among us.

It comes about in this manner. First, Theosophy and its doctrines are well received because affording an explanation of the sorrows of life and a partial answer to the query, "Why is there anything?" Then a deeper examination and larger comprehension of the wide-embracing doctrines of Unity, Reincarnation, Karma, the Sevenfold Classification, cause the person to perceive that either a means of reconciling certain old time dogmas and ideas with Theosophy must be found, or the disaster of giving the old ones up must fall on him.

Contemplating the criminal class and laws thereon the mechanical theosophist sees that perhaps the retaliatory law of Moses must be abandoned if the *modus vivendi* is not found. Ah! of course, are not men agents for karma? Hence the criminal who has murdered may be executed, may be violently thrust out of life, because that is his karma. Besides, Society must be protected. You cite the bearing on this of the subtile, inner, living nature of man. The mechanical theosophist necessarily must shut his eyes to something, so he replies that all of that has no bearing, the criminal did murder and must be murdered; it was his own fault. So at one sweep away goes compassion, and, as well, any scientific view of criminals and sudden death, in order that there may be a retaliatory Mosaic principle, which is really bound up in our personal selfish natures.

Our naturalistic mechanician in the philosophy of life then finds quite a satisfaction. Why, of course, being in his own opinion a karmic agent he has the right to decide when he shall act as such. He will be a conscious agent. And so he executes karma upon his fellows according to his own desires and opinions; but he will not give to the beggar because that has been shown to encourage mendicity, nor would he rescue the drunken woman from the gutter because that is her fault and karma to be there. He assumes certainly to act justly, and perhaps in his narrowness of mind he thinks he is doing so, but real justice is not followed because it is unknown to him, being bound up in the long, invisible karmic streams of himself and his victim. However, he has saved his old theories and yet calls himself a theosophist.

Then again the mechanical view, being narrow and of necessity held by those who have no native knowledge of the occult, sees but the mechanical, outer operations of karma. Hence the subtile relation of parent and child, not only on this plane but on all the hidden planes of nature, is ignored. Instead of seeing that the child is of that parent just because of karma and for definite purposes; and that parentage is not merely for bringing an ego into this life but for wider and greater reasons; the mechanical and naturalistic theosophist is delighted to find that his Theosophy allows one to ignore the relation, and even to curse a parent, because parentage is held to be merely a door into life and nothing more.

Mechanical Theosophy is just as bad as that form of Christianity which permits a man to call his religion the religion of love, while he at the same time may grasp, retaliate, be selfish, and sanction his government's construction of death-dealing appliances and in going to war, although Jesus was opposed to both. Mechanical Theosophy would not condemn — as Christianity does not — those missionaries of Jesus who, finding themselves in danger of death in a land where the people do not want them, appeal to their government for warships, for soldiers, guns and forcible protection in a territory they do not own. It was the mechanical view of Christianity that created an Inquisition. This sort of religion has driven out the true religion of Jesus, and the mechanical view of our doctrines will, if persisted in, do the same for Theosophy.

Our philosophy of life is one grand whole, every part necessary and fitting into every other part. Every one of its doctrines can and must be carried to its ultimate conclusion. Its ethical application must proceed similarly. If it conflict with old opinions those must be cast off. It can never conflict with true morality. But it will with many views touching our dealings with one another. The spirit of Theosophy must be sought for; a sincere application of its principles to life and act should be made. Thus mechanical

Theosophy, which inevitably leads — as in many cases it already has — to a negation of brotherhood, will be impossible, and instead there will be a living, actual Theosophy. This will then raise in our hearts the hope that at least a small nucleus of Universal Brotherhood may be formed before we of this generation are all dead.

The Path, November 1895

ADVANTAGES AND DISADVANTAGES IN LIFE

That view of one's Karma which leads to a bewailing of the unkind fate which has kept advantages in life away from us, is a mistaken estimate of what is good and what is not good for the soul. It is quite true that we may often find persons surrounded with great advantages but who make no corresponding use of them or pay but little regard to them. But this very fact in itself goes to show that the so-called advantageous position in life is really not good nor fortunate in the true and inner meaning of those words. The fortunate one has money and teachers, ability, and means to travel and fill the surroundings with works of art, with music and with ease. But these are like the tropical airs that enervate the body; these enervate the character instead of building it up. They do not in themselves tend to the acquirement of any virtue whatever but rather to the opposite by reason of the constant steeping of the senses in the subtle essences of the sensuous world. They are like sweet things which, being swallowed in quantities, turn to acids in the inside of the body. Thus they can be seen to be the opposite of good Karma.

What then is good Karma and what bad? The all embracing and sufficient answer is this:

Good Karma is that kind which the Ego desires and requires; bad, that which the Ego neither desires nor requires.

And in this the Ego, being guided and controlled by law, by justice, by the necessities of upward evolution, and not by fancy or selfishness or revenge or ambition, is sure to choose the earthly habitation that is most likely, out of all possible of selection, to give a Karma for the real advantage in the end. In this light then, even the lazy, indifferent life of one born rich as well as that of one born low and wicked is right.

When we, from this plane, inquire into the matter, we see that the "advantages" which one would seek were he looking for the strengthening of character, the unloosing of soul force and energy, would be called by the selfish and personal world "disadvantages." Struggle is needed for the gaining of strength; buffeting adverse eras is for the gaining of depth; meagre opportunities may be used for acquiring fortitude; poverty should breed generosity.

The middle ground in all this, and not the extreme, is what we speak of. To be born with the disadvantage of drunken, diseased parents, in the criminal portion of the community, is a punishment which constitutes a wait on the road of evolution. It is a necessity generally because the Ego has drawn about itself in a former life some tendencies which cannot be eliminated in any other way. But we should not forget that sometimes, often in the grand total, a pure, powerful Ego incarnates in just such awful surroundings, remaining good and pure all the time, and staying there for the purpose of uplifting and helping others.

But to be born in extreme poverty is not a disadvantage. Jesus said well when, repeating what many a sage had said before, he described the difficulty experienced by the rich man in entering heaven. If we look at life from the narrow point of view of those who say there is but one earth and after it either eternal heaven or hell, then poverty will be regarded as a great disadvantage and something to be avoided. But seeing that we have many lives to live, and that they will give us all needed opportunity for building up character, we must admit that poverty is not, in itself, necessarily bad Karma. Poverty has no natural tendency to engender selfishness, but wealth requires it.

A sojourn for everyone in a body born to all the pains, deprivations and miseries of modern poverty, is good and just. Inasmuch as the present state of civilization with all its horrors of poverty, of crime, of disease, of wrong relations almost everywhere, has grown out of the past, in which we were workers, it is just that we should experience it all at some point in our career. If some person who now pays no need to the misery of men and women should next life be plunged into one of the slums of our cities for rebirth, it would imprint on the soul the misery of such a situation. This would lead later on to compassion and care for others. For, unless we experience the effects of a state of life we cannot understand or appreciate it from a mere description. The personal part involved in this may not like it as a future prospect, but if the Ego decides that the next personality shall be there then all will be an advantage and not a disadvantage.

If we look at the field of operation in us of the so-called

advantages of opportunity, money, travel and teachers we see at once that it all has to do with the brain and nothing else. Languages, archaeology, music, satiating sight with beauty, eating the finest food, wearing the best clothes, travelling to many places and thus infinitely varying impressions on ear and eye; all these begin and end in the brain and not in the soul or character. As the brain is a portion of the unstable, fleeting body the whole phantasmagoria disappears from view and use when the note of death sends its awful vibration through the physical form and drives out the inhabitant. The wonderful central master-ganglion disintegrates, and nothing at all is left but some faint aromas here and there depending on the actual love within for any one pursuit or image or sensation. Nothing left of it all but a few tendencies — *skandhas*, not of the very best. The advantages then turn out in the end to be disadvantages altogether. But imagine the same brain and body not in places of ease, struggling for a good part of life, doing their duty and not in a position to please the senses: this experience will burn in, stamp upon, carve into the character, more energy, more power and more fortitude. It is thus through the ages that great characters are made. The other mode is the mode of the humdrum average which is nothing after all, as yet, but an animal.

The Path, July 1895

HOW SHOULD WE TREAT OTHERS?

The subject relates to our conduct toward and treatment of our fellows, including in that term all people with whom we have any dealings. No particular mode of treatment is given by Theosophy. It simply lays down the law that governs us in all our acts, and declares the consequences of those acts. It is for us to follow the line of action which shall result first in harmony now and forever, and second, in the reduction of the general sum of hate and opposition in thought or act which now darkens the world.

The great law which Theosophy first speaks of is the law of karma, and this is the one which must be held in view in considering the question. Karma is called by some the "law of ethical causation," but it is also the law of action and reaction; and in all departments of nature the reaction is equal to the action, and sometimes the reaction from the unseen but permanent world seems to be much greater than the physical act or word would appear to warrant on the physical plane. This is because the hidden force on the unseen plane was just as strong and powerful as the reaction is seen by us to be. The ordinary view takes in but half of the facts in any such case and judges wholly by superficial observation.

If we look at the subject only from the point of view of the person who knows not of Theosophy and of the nature of man, nor of the forces Theosophy knows to be operating all the time, then the reply to the question will be just the same as the everyday man makes. That is, that he has certain rights he must and will and ought to protect; that he has property he will and may keep and use any way he pleases; and if a man injure him he ought to and will resent it; that if he is insulted by word or deed he will at once fly not only to administer punishment on the offender, but also try to reform, to admonish, and very often to give that offender up to the arm of the law; that if he knows of a criminal he will denounce him to the police and see that he has meted out to him the punishment provided by the law of man. Thus in everything he will proceed as is the custom and as is thought to be the right way by those who live under the Mosaic retaliatory law.

But if we are to inquire into the subject as Theosophists, and as Theosophists who know certain laws and who insist on the absolute sway of karma, and as people who know what the real constitution of man is, then the whole matter takes on, or ought to take on, a wholly different aspect.

The untheosophical view is based on separation, the Theosophical upon unity absolute and actual. Of course if Theosophists talk of unity but as a dream or a mere metaphysical thing, then they will cease to be Theosophists, and be mere professors, as the Christian world is today, of a code not followed. If we are separate one from the other the world is right and resistance is a duty, and the failure to condemn those who offend is a distinct breach of propriety, of law, and of duty. But if we are all united as a physical and psychical fact, then the act of condemning, the fact of resistance, the insistence upon rights on all occasions — all of which means the entire lack of charity and mercy — will bring consequences as certain as the rising of the sun tomorrow.

What are those consequences, and why are they?

They are simply this, that the real man, the entity, the thinker, will react back on you just exactly in proportion to the way you act to him, and this reaction will be in another life, if not now, and even if now felt will still return in the next life.

The fact that the person whom you condemn, or oppose, or judge seems now in this life to deserve it for his acts in this life, does not alter the other fact that his nature will react against you when the time comes. The reaction is a law not subject to nor altered by any sentiment on your part. He may have, truly, offended you and even hurt you, and done that which in the eye of man is blameworthy, but all this does not have anything to do with the dynamic fact that if you arouse his enmity by your condemnation or judgment there will be a reaction on you, and consequently on the whole of society in any century when the reaction takes place. This is the law and the fact as given by the Adepts, as told by all sages, as reported by those who have seen the inner side of nature, as taught by our philosophy and easily provable by anyone who will take the trouble to examine carefully. Logic and small facts of one day or one life, or arguments on lines laid down by men of the world, who do not know the real power and place of thought nor the real nature of man, cannot sweep this away. After all argument and all logic it will remain. The logic used against it is always lacking in certain premises based on facts, and while seeming to be good logic, because the missing facts are unknown to the logician, it is false logic. Hence an appeal to logic that ignores facts which we know are certain is of no use in this inquiry. And the ordinary argument always uses a number of assumptions which are destroyed by the actual inner facts about thought, about karma, about the reaction by the inner man.

The Master "K.H.," once writing to Mr. Sinnett in *The Occult World*, and speaking for his whole order and not for himself only, distinctly wrote that the man who goes to denounce a criminal or an offender works not with nature and harmony but against both, and that such act tends to destruction instead of construction. Whether the act be large or small, whether it be the denunciation of a criminal, or only your own insistence on rules or laws or rights, does not alter the matter or take it out of the rule laid down by that Adept. For the only difference between the acts mentioned is a difference of degree alone; the act is the same in kind as the violent denunciation of a criminal. Either this Adept was right or wrong. If wrong, why do we follow the philosophy laid down by him and his messenger, and concurred in by all the sages and teachers of the past? If right, why this swimming in an adverse current, as he said himself, why this attempt to show that we can set aside karma and act as we please without consequences following us to the end of time? I know not. I prefer to follow the Adept, and especially so when I see that what he says is in line with facts in nature and is a certain conclusion from the system of philosophy I have found in Theosophy.

I have never found an insistence on my so-called rights at all necessary. They preserve themselves, and it must be true if the law of karma is the truth that no man offends against me unless I in the past have offended against him.

In respect to man, karma has no existence without two or more persons being considered. You act, another person is affected, karma follows. It follows on the thought of each and not on the act, for the other person is moved to thought by your act. Here are two sorts of karma, yours and his, and both are intermixed.

There is the karma or effect on you of your own thought and act, the result on you of the other person's thought; and there is the karma on or with the other person consisting of the direct result of your act and his thoughts engendered by your act and thought. This is all permanent. As affecting you there may be various effects. If you have condemned, for instance, we may mention some: *(a)* the increased tendency in yourself to indulge in condemnation, which will remain and increase from life to life; *(b)* this will at last in you change into violence and all that anger and condemnation may naturally lead to; *(c)* an opposition to you is set up in the other person, which will remain forever until one day both suffer for it, and this may be in a tendency in the other person in any subsequent life to do you harm and hurt you in the million ways possible in life, and often also unconsciously. Thus it may all widen out and affect the whole body of society. Hence no matter how justifiable it may seem to you to condemn or denounce or punish another, you set up cause for sorrow in the whole race that must work out some day. And you must feel it.

The opposite conduct, that is, entire charity, constant forgiveness, wipes out the opposition from others, expends the old enmity and at the same time makes no new similar causes. Any other sort of thought or conduct is sure to increase the sum of hate in the world, to make cause for sorrow, to continually keep up the crime and misery in the world. Each man can for himself decide which of the two ways is the right one to adopt.

Self-love and what people call self-respect may shrink from following the Adept's view I give above, but the Theosophist who wishes to follow the law and reduce the general sum of hate will know how to act and to think, for he will follow the words of the Master of H.P.B. who said: "Do not be ever thinking of yourself and forgetting that there are others; for you have no karma of your own, but the karma of each one is the karma of all." And these words were sent by H.P.B. to the American Section and called by her words of wisdom, as they seem also to me to be, for they accord with law. They hurt the *personality* of the nineteenth century, but the personality is for a day, and soon it will be changed if Theosophists try to follow the law of charity as enforced by the inexorable laws of karma. We should all constantly remember that if we believe in the Masters we should at least try to imitate them in the charity they show for our weakness and faults. In no other way can we hope to reach their high estate, for by beginning thus we set up a tendency which will one day perhaps bring us near to their development; by not beginning we put off the day forever.

The Path, February 1896

AM I MY BROTHER'S KEEPER?

Many students, in their search for light, find divers problems presented to them for solution; questions so puzzling from the contradictory aspects which they present, that the true course is difficult of attainment for those who seek Right Living.

One of these questions, Is it our duty to interfere if we see a wrong being done? arises.

The question of duty is one that can be decided fully only by each individual himself. No code of laws or table of rules unchanging and inflexible will be given, under which all must act, or find duty.

We are so ignorant or so newly acquainted with a portion of the Divine Will that generally we are poorly fitted to declare decisively what is wrong, or evil.

Each man is the law unto himself — the law as to right and wrong, good and evil. No other individual may violate the law of that man, any more than any other law, without producing the inevitable result, the penalty of an infracted law.

I dare not declare that any one thing or course is evil in *another*. For me it may be evil. I am not wise enough to know what it is for another. Only the Supreme knows, for He only can read the heart, the mind, the soul of each. "Thou shalt not judge," saith the sacred writing.

My duty is clear in many places, but in the performing of it I may neither act as a judge or hold animosity, anger, or disgust.

Were a man to abuse an animal, surely I must interfere to prevent suffering to the helpless, dumb and weak, for so we are enjoined. This done, my duty lies in helping my brother, for he knew not what he did.

My aim is to find Wisdom, and my duty, to do away with ignorance wherever it is encountered. His act was caused by ignorance. Were a man to abuse wife or child through unwise use of wine or drug truly it is my duty to prevent suffering or sorrow for either wife or child, and also to prevent greater misery — perhaps murder. They are human beings, my fellows. This done, my duty lies toward the man, not in condemnation, but seeking the cause that makes him unwise, strive to alleviate — if not free him from it. He also is my brother.

If men steal, lie, cheat, betray the innocent or are betrayed by the knowing, my duty lies in preventing for others, if I may, sorrow and anguish, pain and want, misery, suicide or bloodshed, which may be, for *others* the result of these acts.

My duty lies in preventing effects such as these from love for and a desire to help all men, not because men's actions seem to me wrong or their courses evil. I know not the causes of their actions, nor all the reasons why they are permitted. How then may I say this or that man is evil, this or that thing is wrong? The *effects* may to *me* seem evil, inasmuch as such appears to be the result for others. Here my duty is to prevent evil to other mortals in the way that seems most wise.

> Finally this is better that one do
> His own task as he may even though he fail,
> Than take tasks not his own, though they seem good.
>
> *Song Celestial (Bhagavat-Gita)*

He who seeks "the small old path" has many duties to perform. His duty to mankind, his family — nature — himself and his creator, but duty here means something very different from that which is conveyed by the time and lip-worn word, *Duty*. Our comprehension of the term is generally based upon society's or man's selfish interpretation. It is quite generally thought that duty means the performance of a series of acts which *others* think *I* ought to perform, whereas, it more truly means the performance of actions by me which *I know* are good for *others,* or the wisest at the moment.

It would be quite dangerous for me to take upon myself the duty of another, either because he told me it was good, or that it was duty. It would be dangerous for him and me if I assumed that which he felt it was good to do, for that is his duty, and cannot be mine. That which is given him to do I cannot do for him. That which is given me to do no living thing can do for me. If I attempt to do another's duty then I assume that which belongs not to me, was not given me. I am a thief, taking that which does not belong to me. My brother consenting thereto becomes an idler, fails to comprehend the lesson, shifts the responsibility, and between us we accomplish nothing.

We are instructed to do good. That is duty. In doing good all that we do is covered, that for which we are here is being accomplished and that is — duty. We are enjoined to do good *where it is safe.* Not safe for ourselves, but safe for the objects toward which our duty points. Often we behold beings suffering great wrong. Our emotions prompt us to rush forward and in some way prevent the continuance of it. Still the wise man knows it is not safe. Were he to do so his efforts would only rouse the antagonism and passions of superior numbers, whose unrestrained and ungoverned wills would culminate in the perpetration of greater wrongs upon the one who already suffers. It is safe to do good, or my duty, after I find how to do it in the way that will not create evil, harm others or beget greater evils.

For him who seeks the upward way there is no duty — for nothing is a duty. He has learned that the word conveys an erroneous meaning when applied to the doings of the Seeker. It implies the performance of that which savors of a task, or a certain required or demanded act necessary before progress is made or other deeds be performed. Of duty, there is none such as this.

He learns to do good and that which appears the wisest at the time, forgetting self so fully that he only knows his doing good to others — forgetting self so far that he forgets to think whether he is doing his duty or not — entering Nirvana to this extent that he does not remember that he is doing his duty. That *for him* is duty.

"Resist not evil," saith one of the Wise. He who said this knew full well his duty, and desired to convey to us knowledge. That he did not mean men to sit idly by while ignorance let slip the dogs of pain, anguish, suffering, want and murder, is surely true. That he did not mean men to kneel in puerile simulation of holiness by the roadside, while their fellow men suffer torture, wrong or abuse, is still more true. That he did not intend a man to sit silently a looker-on while that which is called evil worked its will upon others when by the lifting of a finger, perhaps, its intentions might be thwarted and annulled — is truth itself. These all would be neglect of a portion of the whole duty of man. He who taught that men should "resist not evil" desired them only to forget themselves. Men think that all things which are disagreeable to them, are evil. By resistance he meant complaint, anger and objection to or against the inevitable, disagreeable or sorrowful things of life, that come to self, and he *did not* mean man to go forth in the guise of a martyr, hugging these same penalties to his bosom while he proclaims himself thereby the possessor of the magic *pass word* (which he will never own and which is never uttered in that way): *I have Suffered.*

If men revile, persecute or wrong one, why resist? Perhaps it is evil, but so long as it affects one's-self only, it is no great matter. If want, sorrow or pain come to one why resist or cry out? In the resistance or war against them we create greater evils. Coming to one's-self, they should have little weight, while at the same time they carry invaluable lessons in their hands. Rightly studied they cause one to forget himself in the desire to assist others when similarly placed, and the Lotus of duty — or love for man — to bloom out of the Nile mire of life. Resist not evil, for it is inseparable from life. It is our duty to live, and accept uncomplainingly, all of life. Resist not evil, but rather learn of it all the good which in reality it only veils.

Seek in it, as well as in the gleaming good, for *the Mystery*, and there will come forth from both the self-same form upon whose forehead is written "Duty," which being interpreted, meaneth efforts for the good of all *other* men, and over whose heart is written: "I am my brother's keeper."

The Path, August 1887   AMERICAN MYSTIC

FRIENDS OR ENEMIES
IN THE FUTURE

The fundamental doctrines of Theosophy are of no value unless they are applied to daily life. To the extent to which this application goes they become living truths, quite different from intellectual expressions of doctrine. The mere intellectual grasp may result in spiritual pride, while the living doctrine becomes an entity through the mystic power of the human soul. Many great minds have dwelt on this. Saint Paul wrote:

> Though I speak with the tongues of men and of angels and have not charity, I am become as sounding brass or a tinkling cymbal. And though I have the gift of prophecy and understand all mysteries and all knowledge, and though I have all faith so that I could remove mountains, and have not charity, I am nothing. And though I bestow all my goods to feed the poor, and though I give my body to be burned, and have not charity, it profiteth me nothing.

The Voice of the Silence, expressing the views of the highest schools of occultism, asks us to step out of the sunlight into the shade so as to make more room for others, and declares that those whom we help in this life will help us in our next one.

Buttresses to these are the doctrines of Karma and Reincarnation. The first shows that we must reap what we sow, and the second that we come back in the company of those with whom we lived and acted in other lives. St. Paul was in complete accord with all other occultists, and his expressions above given must be viewed in the light Theosophy throws on all similar writings. Contrasted with charity, which is love of our fellows, are all the possible virtues and acquirements. These are all nothing if charity be absent. Why? Because they die with the death of the uncharitable person; their value is naught, and that being is reborn without friend and without capacity.

This is of the highest importance to the earnest Theosophist, who may be making the mistake of obtaining intellectual benefits, but remains uncharitable. The fact that we are now working in the Theosophical movement means that we did so in other lives, must do so again, and, still more important, that those who are now with us will be reincarnated in our company on our next rebirth.

Shall those whom we now know or whom we are destined to know before this life ends be our friends or enemies, our aiders or obstructors in that coming life? And what will make them hostile or friendly to us then? Not what we shall say or do to and for them in the future life. For no man becomes your friend in a present life by reason of present acts alone. He was your friend, or you his, before in a previous life. Your present acts but revive the old friendship, renew the ancient obligation.

Was he your enemy before, he will be now even though you do him service now, for these tendencies last always more than three lives. They will be more and still more our aids if we increase the bond of friendship of today by charity. Their tendency to enmity will be one-third lessened in every life if we persist in kindness, in love, in charity now. And that charity is not a gift of money, but charitable thought for every weakness, to every failure.

Our future friends or enemies, then, are those who are with us and to be with us in the present. If they are those who now seem inimical, we make a grave mistake and only put off the day of reconciliation three more lives if we allow ourselves today to be deficient in charity for them. We are annoyed and hindered by those who actively oppose as well as others whose mere looks, temperament, and unconscious action fret and disturb us. Our code of justice to ourselves, often but petty personality, incites us to rebuke them, to criticise, to attack. It is a mistake for us to so act. Could we but glance ahead to next life, we would see these for whom we now have but scant charity crossing the plain of that life with ourselves and ever in our way, always hiding the light from us. But change our present attitude, and that new life to come would show these bores and partial enemies and obstructors helping us, aiding our every effort. For Karma may give them then greater opportunities than ourselves and better capacity.

Is any Theosophist, who reflects on this, so foolish as to continue now, if he has the power to alter himself, a course that will breed a crop of thorns for his next life's reaping? We should continue our charity and kindness to our friends whom it is easy to wish to help, but for those whom we naturally dislike, who are our bores now, we ought to take especial pains to aid and carefully toward them cultivate a feeling of love and charity. This adds interest to our Karmic investment. The opposite course, as surely as sun rises and water runs down hill, strikes interest from the account and enters a heavy item on the wrong side of life's ledger.

And especially should the whole Theosophical organization act on the lines laid down by St. Paul and *The Voice of the Silence.* For Karmic tendency is an unswerving law. It compels us to go on in this movement of thought and doctrine; it will bring back to reincarnation all in it now. Sentiment cannot move the law one inch; and though that emotion might seek to rid us of the presence of these men and women we presently do not fancy or approve — and there are many such in our ranks for every one — the law will place us again in company with friendly tendency increased or hostile feeling diminished, just as we now create the one or prevent the other. It was the aim of the founders of the Society to arouse tendency to future friendship; it ought to be the object of all our members.

What will you have? In the future life, enemies or friends?

The Path, January 1893   EUSEBIO URBAN

ON THE FUTURE:
A FEW REFLECTIONS

Although I am an American citizen, the place of my birth was in Ireland, and in what I am about to say I cannot be accused of Columbiamania, for no matter how long might be my life I could never be an American. For that perhaps it is right, since it is compulsory, to wait for some distant incarnation.

Now, either H.P.B. was right or she was wrong in what she says in the *Secret Doctrine* about the future of America. If wrong, then all this may be dismissed as idle speculation. But, if right, then all thoughtful Theosophists must take heed, weigh well, mentally appropriate and always remember what are her words as well as the conclusions to which they lead.

In the first pages of the second volume she speaks of five great Continents. *First*, the Imperishable Sacred Land [this is at the North Pole, *W.Q.J.*]; *second*, the Hyperborean, now part of it is in Northern Asia; *third*, Lemuria, sunk long ago, but leaving some remains, islands, the points of high mountain ranges; *fourth*, Atlantis, presumably in the Atlantic Ocean, now below the level of the water, but with perhaps Teneriffe and Atlas as reminders; and *fifth*, "was America."

From a survey of the book, digging in notes and culling from the text here and there, the conclusion is irresistible that although the present America is not the actual Continent as *it is to be*, it is a portion of it; and certainly is now the nursery for the race that will in the future occupy the *sixth* Continent, which for the sixth Great Root-Race will emerge from the waters. Where? Perhaps when the present America has been split up by tremendous cataclysms, leaving here and there large pieces on its western side, it is in the Pacific Ocean that the great mass of the new one will come up from the long sleep below the sea. Rightly then will the great far western ocean have been named *Pacific*, for that Race will not be given to contest nor hear of wars or rumours of war, since it will be too near the seventh, whose mission it must be to attain to the consummation, to seize and hold the Holy Grail.

Turn to page 444 and onward of the second volume. Read there that the Americans have become in only three hundred years a primary race *pro tem.*, in short, the germs of the sixth sub-race, to blossom in a few more centuries into the pioneers of that one which must succeed to the present European fifth sub-race in all its characteristics. Then after about 25,000 years, which you will note is meant for a great sidereal cycle of a little over that length of time, this new race will prepare for the seventh sub-race. Catalysms will then fall upon you; lands and nations will be swept away, first of all being the European, including the British Isles — if not gone before — and then parts of both North and South America. And how puny, mongrel, indeed, will be the remains of the scientists of today, great masters of microbes now, but then to be looked upon as strange remains of the Nineteenth Century, when, as the people will tell each other then, so many, with Truth before them, laughed at it and stoned its apostles, dancing a fantastic dance meanwhile around the altar of invisible matter.

It seems as if some power, deliberately planning, had selected North and South America for the place where a new primary root-race should be begun. These two continents were evidently the seats of ancient races and not the habitat of wild undeveloped men. The red man of the Northern one has all the appearance and beliefs of a once great race. He believes in one God, a Devachan of happy hunting after death. Some tribes have diagrams of how the world was formed and peopled, that strangely resemble the Hindu cosmogony, and their folklore bears deep marks of having come down from an older and better time. Following the course of exploration southwards, we find accumulating evidences all the way of a prior civilization now gone with the cyclic wave which brought it up. Central America is crowded with remains in stone and brick; and so on south still we discover similar proofs. In course of time these continents became what might be called arable land, lying waiting, recuperating, until the European streams of men began to pour upon it. The Spanish overflowed South America and settled California and Mexico; the English, French, and Spanish took the North, and later all nations came, so that now in both continents nearly every race is mixed and still mixing. Chinese even have married women of European blood; Hindus are also here; the ancient Parsi race has its representatives; the Spanish mixed with the aborigines, and the slaveholders with the Africans.

I doubt not but that some one from every race known to us has been here and has left, within the last two hundred years, some impression through mixture of blood.

But the last remnants of the fifth Continent, America, will not disappear until the new race has been some time born. Then a new Dwelling, the sixth Continent, will have appeared over the waters to receive the youth who will tower above us as we do above the pigmies of Africa. But no America as we now know it will exist. Yet these men must be the descendants of the race that is now rising here. Otherwise our philosophy is all wrong. So then, in America now is forming the new sub-race, and in this land was founded the present Theosophical Society: two matters of great importance. It was to the United States, observe, that the messenger of the Masters came, although Europe was just as accessible for the enterprise set on foot. Later, this messenger went to India and then to Europe, settling down in the British Isles. All of this is of importance in our reflections. For why in America at first does she begin the movement, and why end her part of it in England? One might be led to ask why was not an effort made at all costs to give the last impulse outwardly in the land of promise where she began the work?

Do not imagine for one moment, O ye English brothers of mine, that London was selected for this because the beauties of your island called her, or for that she had decided at the finish that after all a mistake had been made in not going there first. It was all out of stern necessity, with a wisdom derived from many other heads, having in view the cycles as they sweep resistlessly forward. The point where the great energy is started, the centre of force, is the more important, and not the place at which it is ended. And this remains true, no matter how essential the place of ending may be in the scheme. What, do you suppose India is not as important? and would not that land have offered seemingly a better spot than all for the beginning of the *magnum opus*? Adepts do not make mistakes like that.

America's discovery is ascribed to Christopher Columbus. Although it is doubted, yet no one doubts that the Spanish people did the most at first in peopling it, meanwhile working off some old and making some new Karma, by killing many of the aborigines. Thus it is that doomed people rush on to their doom, even as the troops of insects, animals and men were seen by Arjuna to rush into Krishna's flaming mouths. But later came the sturdy stock from England, who, in the greatest nation, the most enduring on this continent, have left their impress indelibly in the people, in its laws, in its constitution, its customs, its literature and language. Perhaps England and Ireland are the gateways for the Egos who incarnate here in the silent work of making a new race. Maybe there is some significance in the fact that more lines of steamships conveying human freight come to the United States from England, passing Ireland on the way as the last seen land of the old world, than from anywhere else. The deeds of men, the enterprises of merchants, and the wars of soldiers all follow implicitly a law that is fixed in the stars, and while they copy the past they ever symbolize the future.

Did H.P.B. only joke when she wrote in her book that Ireland is an ancient Atlantean remnant, and England a younger Isle, whose rising from the sea was watched by wise men from Erin's shore? Perhaps the people of that old land may have an important influence in the new race of America. It would appear from comparison that they might have had, and probably will in the future. Perhaps, politically, since many expect social disturbances in America. In such a case any student of character will admit that the Irish, ignorant or not, will stand for law and order — for her sons are not battling here with an ancient foe. Why, too, by strange freak of fate is the great stone of destiny in Westminster Abbey fixed under the coronation chair on which the Queen was crowned? Let us also be informed if there be any finger-shadow pointing to the future in the fact that England's Queen, crowned over that stone,* is Empress of India, from which we claim the Aryans came, and where their glorious long-forgotten knowledge is preserved? Her name is Victory. It is the victory for "the new order of Ages"; and that new order began in America, its advent noted and cut on the as yet unused obverse side of the present seal of the United States Government. A victory in the union of the Egos from East and West; for England stretches one hand over to the home of the new race, which she can never own, with the other

---

* It is an interesting fact that in India there is an important ceremony called "mounting the stone."

governing India, and completes the circuit. It may be a fleeting picture, perhaps to be wiped out for a while in a stream of blood, but such is the way the cycles roll and how we may learn to read the future. For England's destiny is not complete, nor has the time struck. None of us hug foolish delusions too long, and even if Ireland were once a most sacred place, that is no reason why we should want to go there. For in America those whose Karma has led them there will work for the same end and brotherhood as others left in India and Europe. The dominant language and style of thought in America is English, albeit transforming itself every day. It is there that silently the work goes on; there European fathers and mothers have gone, establishing currents of attraction that will inevitably and unceasingly draw into reincarnation Egos similar to themselves. And the great forward and backward rush is completed by the retarded Egos as they die out of other nations, coming meanwhile into flesh again among the older races left behind.

*   *   *   *

At least such seemed the view while the clouds lifted — and then once more there was silence.

Lucifer, March 1892

MUSINGS ON THE
TRUE THEOSOPHIST'S PATH

The way of inward peace is in all things to conform to the pleasure and disposition of the Divine Will. Such as would have all things succeed and come to pass according to their own fancy, are not come to know this way; and therefore lead a harsh and bitter life; always restless and out of humor, without treading the way of peace."

Know then Oh Man, that he who seeks the hidden way, can only find it through the door of life. In the hearts of all, at some time, there arises the desire for knowledge. He who thinks his desire will be fulfilled, as the little bird in the nest, who has only to open his mouth to be fed, will very truly be disappointed.

In all nature we can find no instance where effort of some kind is not required. We find there is a natural result from such effort. He who would live the life or find wisdom can only do so by continued effort. If one becomes a student, and learns to look partially within the veil, or has found within his own being something that is greater than his outer self, it gives no authority for one to sit down in idleness or fence himself in from contact with the world. Because one sees the gleam of the light ahead he cannot say to his fellow "I am holier than thee" or draw the mantle of seclusion around himself.

The soul develops like the flower, in God's sunlight, and unconsciously to the soil in which it grows. Shut out the light and the soil grows damp and sterile, the flower withers or grows pale and sickly. Each and every one is here for a good and wise reason. If we find partially *the why* we are here, then is there the more reason that we should by intelligent contact with life, seek in it the farther elucidation of the problem. It is not the study of ourselves so much, as the thought for others that opens this door. The events of life and their causes lead to knowledge. They must be studied when they are manifested in daily life.

There is no idleness for the Mystic. He finds his daily life among the roughest and hardest of the labors and trials of the world perhaps, but goes his way with smiling face and joyful heart, nor grows too sensitive for association with his fellows, nor so extremely spiritual as to forget that some other body is perhaps hungering for food.

It was said by one who pretended to teach the mysteries "It is needful that I have a pleasant location and beautiful surroundings." He who is a true Theosoph will wait for nothing of the sort, either before teaching, or what is first needful, learning. It would perhaps, be agreeable, but if the Divine Inspiration comes only under those conditions, then indeed is the Divine afar from the most of us. He only can be a factor for good or teach how to approach the way, who forgetting his own surroundings, strives to beautify and illumine those of others. The effort must be for the good of others, not the gratifying of our own senses, or love for the agreeable or pleasant.

Giving thought to self will most truly prevent and overthrow your aims and objects, particularly when directed toward the occult.

Again there arises the thought "I am a student, a holder of a portion of the mystic lore." Insidiously there steals in the thought "Behold I am a little more than other men, who have not penetrated so far." Know then oh man, that you are not as great even as they. He who thinks he is wise is the most ignorant of men, and he who begins to *believe* he is wise is in greater danger than any other man who lives.

You think, oh man, that because you have obtained a portion of occult knowledge, that it entitles you to withdraw from contact with the rest of mankind. It is not so. If you have obtained true knowledge it forces you to meet all men not only half way, but more than that to seek them. It urges you not to retire but, seeking contact, to plunge into the misery and sorrow of the world, and with your cheering word, if you have no more (the Mystic has little else) strive to lighten the burden for some struggling soul.

You dream of fame. We know no such thing as fame. He who seeks the upward path finds that all is truth; that evil is the good gone astray. Why should we ask for fame? It is only the commendation of those we strive to help.

Desire neither notice, fame or wealth. Unknown you are in retirement. Being fameless you are undisturbed in your seclusion, and can walk the broad face of the earth fulfilling your duty, as commanded, unrecognized.

If the duty grows hard, or you faint by the way, be not discouraged, fearful or weary of the world. Remember that "Thou may'st look for silence in tumult, solitude in company, light in darkness, forgetfulness in pressures, vigor in despondency, courage in fear, resistance in temptation, peace in war, and quiet in tribulation."

II

> Work as those work who are ambitious. — Respect life as those do who desire it. — Be happy as those are who live for happiness.
>
> *Light on the Path*

We are tried in wondrous ways, and in the seemingly unimportant affairs of life, there often lie the most dangerous of the temptations.

Labor, at best, is frequently disagreeable owing either to mental or physical repugnance. When he who seeks the upward path, begins to find it, labor grows more burdensome, while at the time, he is, owing to his physical condition, not so well fitted to struggle with it. This is all true, but there must be no giving in to it. It must be forgotten. He *must work,* and if he cannot have the sort he desires or deems best suited to him, then must he take and perform that which presents itself. It is that which he most needs. It is not intended either, that he do it to have it done. It is intended that he work as if it was the object of his life, as if his whole heart was in it. Perhaps he may be wise enough to know that there is something else, or that the future holds better gifts for him, still this also must to all intents be forgotten, while he takes up his labor, as if there were no tomorrow.

Remember that life is the outcome of the Ever-Living. If you have come to comprehend a little of the mystery of life, and can value its attractions according to their worth; these are no reasons why you should walk forth with solemn countenance to blight the enjoyments of other men. Life to them is as real, as the mystery is to you. Their time will come as yours has, so hasten it for them, if you can, by making life brighter, more joyous, better.

If it be your time to fast, put on the best raiment you have, and go forth, not as one who fasts, but as one who lives for life.

Do your sighing and crying within you. If you can not receive the small events of life and their meanings without crying them out to all the world, think you that you are fitted to be trusted with the mysteries?

The doing away with one or certain articles of diet, *in itself,* will not open the sealed portals. If this contained the key, what wise beings must the beasts of the field be, and what a profound Mystic must Nebuchadnezzar have been, after he was "turned out to grass!"

There are some adherents of a faith, which has arisen in the land, who deem it wise to cast away all things that are distasteful to them; to cut asunder the ties of marriage because they deem it will interfere with their spiritual development, or because the other pilgrim is not progressed enough. Brothers, there lives not the man who is wise enough to sit as a judge upon the spiritual development of any living being. He is not only unwise but blasphemous who says to another: "Depart! you impede my exalted spiritual development."

The greatest of all truths lies frequently in plain sight, or veiled in contraries. The impression has gone abroad that the Adept or the Mystic of high degree, has only attained his station by forsaking the association of his fellow creatures or refusing the marriage tie. It is the belief of very wise Teachers that all men who had risen to the highest degrees of Initiation, have at some time passed through the married state. Many men, failing in the trials, have ascribed their failure to being wedded, precisely as that other coward, Adam, after being *the first transgressor* cried out "It was Eve."

One of the most exalted of the Divine Mysteries lies hidden here — therefore, Oh Man, it is wise to cherish that which holds so much of God and seek to know its meaning; not by dissolution and cutting asunder, but by binding and strengthening the ties. Our most Ancient Masters knew of this and Paul also speaks of it. (Ephesians v.32.)

Be patient, kindly and wise, for perhaps in the next moment of life, the light will shine out upon thy companion, and you discover that you are but a blind man, claiming to see. Remember this, that you own not one thing in this world. Your wife is but a gift, your children are but loaned to you. All else you possess is given to you only while you use it wisely. Your body is not yours, for Nature claims it as her property. Do you not think, Oh Man, that it is the height of arrogance for you to sit in judgment upon any other created thing, while you, a beggar, are going about in a borrowed robe?

If misery, want and sorrow are thy portion for a time, be happy that it is not death. If it is death be happy there is no more of life.

You would have wealth, and tell of the good you would do with it. Truly will you lose your way under these conditions. It is quite probable, that you are as rich as you ever will be, therefore, desire to do good with what you have — and *do it*. If you have nothing, know that it is best and wisest for you. Just so surely as you murmur and complain just so surely will you find that "from him that hath not, shall be taken even that which he hath." This sounds contradictory, but in reality is in most harmonious agreement. Work in life and the Occult are similar; all is the result of your own effort and will. You are not rash enough to believe that you will be lifted up into Heaven like the Prophet of old — but you really hope some one will come along and give you a good shove toward it.

Know then, Disciples, that you only can lift yourselves by your own efforts. When this is done, you may have the knowledge that you will find many to accompany you on your heretofore lonely journey; but neither they or your Teacher will be permitted to push or pull you one step onward.

This is all a very essential part of your preparation and trial for Initiation.

You look and wait for some great and astounding occurrence, to show you that you are going to be permitted to enter behind the veil; that you are to be Initiated. It will never come. He only who studies all things and learns from them, as he finds them, will be permitted to enter, and for him there are no flashing lightnings or rolling thunder. He who enters the door, does so as gently and imperceptibly, as the tide rises in the nighttime.

Live well your life. Seek to realize the meaning of every event. Strive to find the Ever Living and wait for more light. The True Initiate does not fully realize what he is passing through, until his degree is received. If you are striving for light and Initiation, remember this, that your cares will increase, your trials thicken, your family make new demands upon you. He who can understand and pass through these patiently, wisely, placidly — may hope.

III

If you desire to labor for the good of the world, it will be unwise for you to strive to include it all at once in your efforts. If you can help elevate or teach but one soul — that is a good beginning, and more than is given to many.

Fear nothing that is in Nature and visible. Dread no influence exerted by sect, faith, or society. Each and every one of them originated upon the same basis — Truth, or a portion of it at least. You may not assume that you have a greater share than they, it being needful only, that you find all the truth each one possesses. You are at war with none. It is peace you are seeking, therefore it is best that the good in everything is found. For this brings peace.

It has been written that he who lives the Life shall know the doctrine. Few there be who realize the significance of The Life.

It is not by intellectually philosophizing upon it, until reason ceases to solve the problem, nor by listening in ecstatic delight to the ravings of an *Elemental clothed* — whose hallucinations are but the offspring of the Astral — that the life is realized. Nor will it be realized by the accounts of the experiences of other students. For there be some who will not realize Divine Truth itself, when written, unless it be properly punctuated or expressed in flowery flowing words.

Remember this: that as you live your life each day with an uplifted purpose and unselfish desire, each and every event will bear for you a deep significance — an occult meaning — and as you learn their import, so do you fit yourself for higher work.

There are no rose-gardens upon the way in which to loiter about, nor fawning slaves to fan one with golden rods of Ostrich plumes. The Ineffable Light will not stream out upon you every time you may think you have turned up the wick, nor will you find yourself sailing about in an astral body, to the delight of yourself and the astonishment of the rest of the world, simply because you are making the effort to find wisdom.

He who is bound in any way — he who is narrow in his

thoughts — finds it doubly difficult to pass onward. You may equally as well gain wisdom and light in a church as by sitting upon a post while your nails grow through your hands. It is not by going to extremes or growing fanatical in any direction that the life will be realized.

Be temperate in all things, most of all in the condemnation of other men. It is unwise to be intemperate or drunken with wine. It is equally unwise to be drunken with temperance. Men would gain the powers; or the way of working wonders. Do you know, O man, what the powers of the Mystic are? Do you know that for each gift of this kind he gives a part of himself? That it is only with mental anguish, earthly sorrow, and almost his heart's blood, these gifts are gained? Is it true, think you, my brother, that he who truly possesses them desires to sell them at a dollar a peep, or any other price? He who would trade upon these things finds himself farther from his goal than when he was born.

There *are* gifts and powers. Not just such as you have created in your imagination, perhaps. Harken to one of these powers: He who has passed onward to a certain point, finds that the hearts of men lie spread before him as an open book, and from there onward the motives of men are clear. In other words he can read the hearts of men. But not selfishly; should he but once use this knowledge selfishly, the book is closed — and he reads no more. Think you, my brothers, he would permit himself to *sell* a page out of this book?

Time — that which does not exist outside the inner circle of this little world — seems of vast importance to the physical man. There comes to him at times, the thought that he is not making any progress, and that he is receiving nothing from some Mystic source. From the fact that he has the thought that no progress is being made the evidence is gained that he is working onward. Only the dead in living bodies need fear. That which men would receive from Mystic sources is frequently often repeated, and in such a quiet, unobtrusive voice, that he who is waiting to hear it shouted in his ear, is apt to pass on unheeding.

Urge no man to see as yourself, as it is quite possible you may see differently when you awake in the morning. It is wiser to let the matter rest without argument. No man is absolutely convinced by that. It is but blowing your breath against the whirlwind.

It was at one time written over the door: "Abandon Hope, all ye who enter here." It has taken hundreds of years for a few to come to the realization that the wise men had not the slightest desire for the company of a lot of hopeless incurables in the mysteries. There is to be abandoned hope for the gratification of our passions, our curiosities, our ambition or desire for gain. There is also another Hope — the true; and he is a wise man who comes to the knowledge of it. Sister to Patience, they together are the Godmothers of Right Living, and two of the Ten who assist the Teacher.

The Path, August, October 1886,   AMERICAN MYSTIC
February 1887

MAHATMAS AS IDEALS AND FACTS

A visitor from one of the other planets of the solar system who might learn the term *Mahatma* after arriving here would certainly suppose that the etymology of the word undoubtedly inspired the believers in *Mahatmas* with the devotion, fearlessness, hope, and energy which such an ideal should arouse in those who have the welfare of the human race at heart. Such a supposition would be correct in respect to some, but the heavenly visitor after examining all the members of the Theosophical Society could not fail to meet disappointment when the fact was clear to him that many of the believers were afraid of their own ideals, hesitated to proclaim them, were slothful in finding arguments to give reasons for their hope, and all because the wicked and scoffing materialistic world might laugh at such a belief.

The whole sweep, meaning, and possibility of evolution are contained in the word *Mahatma*. *Maha* is 'great,' *Atma* is 'soul,' and both compounded into one mean those great souls who have triumphed before us not because they are made of different stuff and are of some strange family, but just because they are of the human race. Reincarnation, karma, the sevenfold division, retribution, reward, struggle, failure, success, illumination, power, and a vast embracing love for man, all these lie in that single word. The soul emerges from the unknown, begins to work in and with matter, is reborn again and again, makes karma, develops the six vehicles for itself, meets retribution for sin and punishment for mistake, grows strong by suffering, succeeds in bursting through the gloom, is enlightened by the true illumination, grasps power, retains charity, expands with love for orphaned humanity, and thenceforth helps all others who remain in darkness until all may be raised up to the place with the 'Father in Heaven' who is the Higher Self. This would be the argument of the visitor from the distant planet, and he in it would describe a great ideal for all members of a Society such as ours which had its first impulse from some of these very *Mahatmas*.

Without going into any argument further than to say that evolution demands that such beings should exist or there is a gap in the chain — and this position is even held by a man of science like Professor Huxley, who in his latest essays put it in almost as definite language as mine — this article is meant for those who believe in the existence of the *Mahatmas*, whether that faith has arisen of itself or is the result of argument. It is meant also for all classes of the believers, for they are of several varieties. Some believe without wavering; others believe unwaveringly but are afraid to tell of their belief; a few believe, yet are always thinking that they must be able to say they have set eyes on an Adept before they can infuse their belief into others; and a certain number deliberately hide the belief as a sort of individual possession which separates them from the profane mortals who have never heard of the Adepts or who having heard scoff at the notion. To all these I wish to speak. Those unfortunate persons who are ever trying to measure exalted men and sages by the conventional rules of a transition civilization, or who are seemingly afraid of a vast possibility for man and therefore deny, may be well left to themselves and to time, for it is more than likely they will fall into the general belief when it is formed, as it surely will be in the course of no long time. For a belief in *Mahatmas* — whatever name you give the idea — is a common property of the whole race, and all the efforts of all the men of empirical science and dogmatic religion can never kill out the soul's own memory of its past.

We should declare our belief in the Adepts, while at the same time we demand no one's adherence. It is not necessary to give the names of any of the Adepts, for a name is an invention of a family, and but few persons ever think of themselves by name but by the phrase 'I am myself.' To name these beings, then, is no proof, and to seek for mystery names is to invite condemnation for profanation. The ideal without the name is large and grand enough for all purposes.

Some years ago the Adepts wrote and said to H.P.B. and to several persons that more help could be given to the movement in America because the fact of their existence was not concealed from motives of either fear or doubt. This statement of course carries with it by contradistinction the conclusion that where, from fear of schools of science or of religion, the members had not referred much to the belief in *Mahatmas*, the power to help was for some reason inhibited. This is the interesting point, and brings up the question 'Can the power to help of the *Mahatmas* be for any cause inhibited?' The answer is, It can. But why?

All effects on every plane are the result of forces set in motion, and cannot be the result of nothing, but must ever flow from causes in which they are wrapped up. If the channel through which water is meant to flow is stopped up, the water will not run there, but if a clear channel is provided the current will pass forward. Occult help from Masters requires a channel just as much as any other help does, and the fact that the currents to be used are occult makes the need for a channel greater. The persons to be acted on must take part in making the channel or line for the force to act, for if we will not have it they cannot give it. Now as we are dealing with the mind and nature of man, we have to throw out the words which will arouse the ideas connected with the forces we desire to have employed. In this case the words are those which bring up the doctrine of the existence of Adepts, Mahatmas, Masters of wisdom. Hence the value of the declaration of our belief. It arouses dormant ideas in others, it opens up a channel in the mind, it serves to make the conducting lines for the forces to use which the *Mahatmas* wish to give out. Many a young man who could never hope to see great modern professors of science like Huxley and Tyndall and Darwin has been excited to action, moved to self-help, impelled to seek for knowledge, by having heard that such men actually exist and are human beings. Without stopping to ask if the proof of their living in Europe is complete, men have sought to follow their example. Shall we not take advantage of the same law of the human mind and let the vast power of the Lodge work with our assistance and not against our opposition or doubt or fear? Those who are devoted know how they have had unseen help which showed itself in results. Those who fear may take courage, for they will find that not all their fellow beings are devoid of an underlying belief in the possibilities outlined by the doctrine of the existence of the Adepts.

And if we look over the work of the Society we find wherever the members boldly avow their belief and are not afraid to speak of this high ideal, the interest in Theosophy is awake, the work goes on, the people are benefited. To the contrary, where there are constant doubts, ceaseless asking for material proof, incessant fear of what the world or science or friends will think, there the work is dead, the field is not cultivated, and the town or city receives no benefit from the efforts of those who while formally in a universal brotherhood are not living out the great ideal.

Very wisely and as an occultist, Jesus said his followers must give up all and follow him. We must give up the desire to save ourselves and acquire the opposite one — the wish to save others. Let us remember the story in ancient writ of Yudhishthira, who, entering heaven and finding that his dog was not admitted and some of his friends in hell, refused to remain and said that while one creature was out of heaven he would not enter it. This is true devotion, and this joined to an intelligent declaration of belief in the great initiation of the human race will lead to results of magnitude, will call out the forces that are behind, will prevail against hell itself and all the minions of hell now striving to retard the progress of the human soul.

The Path, March 1893

GURU AND CHELA

The first question a man should ask himself (and by 'man' we mean postulants of either sex) is: "When and how did I get a desire to know about chelaship and to become a chela?"; and secondly, "What is a chela, and what chelaship?"

There are many sorts of chelas. There are lay chelas and probationary ones; accepted chelas and those who are trying to fit themselves to be even lay chelas. Any person can constitute himself a lay chela, feeling sure that he may never in this life consciously hear from his guide. Then as to probationary chelas, there is an *invariable* rule that they go upon seven years' trial. These 'trials' do not refer to fixed and stated tests, but to all the events of life and the bearing of the probationer in them. There is no *place* to which applicants can be referred where their request could be made, because these matters do not relate to places and to officials: this is an affair of the inner nature. We *become* chelas; we obtain that position in reality because our inner nature is to that extent opened that it can and will take knowledge: we receive the guerdon at the hands of the Law. . . .

As a general thing, a person of European or American birth has extreme difficulty to contend with. He has no heredity of psychical development to call upon; no known assembly of Masters or Their chelas within reach. His racial difficulties prevent him from easily seeing within himself; he is not introspective by nature. But even he can do much if he purifies his motive, and either naturally possesses or cultivates an ardent and unshakeable faith and devotion — a faith that keeps him a firm believer in the existence of Masters even through years of non-intercourse. They are generous and honest debtors and always repay. How They repay, and when, is not for us to ask. Men may say this requires as blind devotion as was ever asked by any Church. *It does,* but it is a blind devotion to Masters who are Truth itself; to Humanity and to yourself, to your own intuitions and ideals. This devotion to an ideal is also founded upon another thing, which is that a man is hardly ready to be a chela unless he is able to stand *alone* and uninfluenced by other men or events. *For he must stand alone*, and he might as well know this at the beginning as at the end.

There are also certain qualifications which he must possess. These are to be found in *Man: Fragments of Forgotten History*, towards the close of the book, so we will not dwell upon them here.

The question of the general fitness of applicants being disposed of, we come to the still more serious point of the relations of Guru and Chela, or Master and Disciple. We want to know what it really is to be a pupil of such a Teacher.

The relation of Guru and Chela is nothing if it is not a spiritual one. Whatever is merely outward, or formal, as the relation established by mere asking and acceptance, is not spiritual, but formal, and is that which arises between *teacher* and *pupil*. Yet even this latter is not in any way despicable, because the teacher stands to his pupil, in so far as the relation permits, in the same way as the Guru to his Chela. It is a difference of degree; but this difference of degree is what constitutes the distinction between the spiritual and the material, for, passing along the different shadings from the grossest materiality to as far as we can go, we find at last that matter merges into spirit. (We are now speaking, of course, about what is commonly called *matter*, while we well know that in truth the thing thus designated is not really matter, but an enormous illusion which in itself has no existence. The real matter, called *mulaprakriti* by the Hindus, is an invisible thing or substance of which our matter is a representation. The real matter is what the Hermetists called *primordial earth*; for us, an intangible phase of matter. We can easily come to believe that what is usually called *matter* is not really such, inasmuch as we find clairvoyants and nervous people seeing through thick walls and closed doors. Were this *matter*, then they could not see through it. But when an ordinary clairvoyant comes face to face with *primordial matter*, he or she cannot see beyond, but is met by a dead wall more dense than any wall ever built by human hands.)

So from earliest times, among all but modern western people, the teacher was given great reverence by the pupil, and the latter was taught from youth to look upon his preceptor as second only to his father and mother in dignity. It was among these people a great sin, a thing that did one actual harm in his moral being, to be disrespectful to his teacher even in thought. The reason for this lay then, and no less to-day does also lie, in the fact that a long chain of influence extends from the highest spiritual guide who may belong to any man, down through vast numbers of spiritual chiefs, ending at last in the mere teacher of our youth. Or, to restate it in modern reversion of thought, a chain extends up from our teacher or preceptors to the highest spiritual chief in whose ray or descending line one may happen to be. And it makes no difference whatever, in this occult relation, that neither pupil nor final guide may be aware, or admit, that this is the case.

Thus it happens that the child who holds his teacher in reverence, and diligently applies himself accordingly with faith, does no violence to this intangible but mighty chain, and is benefited accordingly, whether he knows it or not. Nor again does it matter that a child has a teacher who evidently gives him a bad system. This is his Karma, and by his reverent and diligent attitude he works it out, and transcends that erstwhile teacher.

This chain of influence is called the *Guruparampara chain*.

The Guru is the *guide* or *readjuster*, and may not always combine the function of teacher with it.

Letters That Have Helped Me, pp. 40-43

THE TELL-TALE PICTURE GALLERY

Although the gallery of pictures about which I now write has long ago been abandoned, and never, since its keepers left the spot where it was, has it been seen there, similar galleries are still to be found in places that one cannot get into until guided to them. They are now secreted in distant and inaccessible spots; in the Himalaya mountains, beyond them, in Tibet, in underground India, and such mysterious localities. The need for reports by spies or for confessions by transgressors is not felt by secret fraternities which possess such strange recorders of the doings, thoughts, and condition of those whom they portray. In the brotherhoods of the Roman Catholic Church or in Free-masonry, no failure to abide by rules could ever be dealt with unless some one reported the delinquent or he himself made a confession. Every day mason after mason breaks both letter and spirit of the vows he made, but, no one knowing or making charges, he remains a mason in good standing. The soldier in camp or field oversteps the strictest rules of discipline, yet if done out of sight of those who could divulge or punish he remains untouched. And in the various religious bodies, the members continually break, either in act or in thought, all the commandments, unknown to their fellows and the heads of the Church, with no loss of standing. But neither the great Roman Church, the Freemasons, nor any religious sect possesses such a gallery as that of which I will try to tell you, one in which is registered every smallest deed and thought.

I do not mean the great Astral Light that retains faithful pictures of all we do, whether we be Theosophists or Scoffers, Catholics or Freemasons, but a veritable collection of simulacrae deliberately constructed so as to specialize one of the many functions of the Astral Light.

It was during one of my talks with the old man who turned into a wandering eye that I first heard of this wonderful gallery, and after his death I was shown the place itself. It was kept on the Sacred Island where of old many weird and magical things existed and events occurred. You may ask why these are not now found there, but you might as well request that I explain why Atlantis sank beneath the wave or why the great Assyrian Empire has disappeared. They have had their day, just as our present boasted civilization will come to its end and be extinguished. Cyclic law cannot be held from its operation, and just as sure as tides change on the globe and blood flows in the body, so sure it is that great doings reach their conclusion and powerful nations disappear.

It was only a few months previous to the old man's death, when approaching dissolution or superior orders, I know not which, caused him to reveal many things and let slip hints as to others. He had been regretting his numerous errors one day, and turning to me said,

"And have you never seen the gallery where your actual spiritual state records itself?"

Not knowing what he meant I replied, "I did not know they had one here."

"Oh yes! it is in the old temple over by the mountain, and the diamond gives more light there than anywhere else."

Fearing to reveal my dense ignorance, not only of what he meant but also of the nature of this gallery, I continued the conversation in a way to elicit more information, and he, supposing I had known of others, began to describe this one. But in the very important part of the description he turned the subject as quickly as he had introduced it, so that I remained a prey to curiosity. And until the day of his death he did not again refer to it. The extraordinary manner of his decease, followed by the weird wandering eye, drove the thought of the pictures out of my head.

But it would seem that the effect of this floating, lonely, intelligent eye upon my character was a shadow or foretoken of my introduction to the gallery. His casual question, in connection with his own shortcomings and the lesson impressed on me by the intensification and concentration of all his nature into one eye that ever wandered about the Island, made me turn my thoughts inward so as to discover and destroy the seeds of evil in myself. Meanwhile all duties in the temple where I lived were assiduously performed. One night after attaining to some humanity of spirit, I fell quietly asleep with the white moonlight falling over the floor, and dreamed that I met the old man again as when alive, and that he asked me if I had yet seen the picture gallery. "No," said I in the dream, "I had forgotten it," awakening then at the sound of my own voice. Looking up, I saw standing in the moonlight a figure of one I had not seen in any of the temples. This being gazed at me with clear, cold eyes, and afar off sounded what I supposed its voice:

"Come with me."

Rising from the bed I went out into the night, following this laconic guide. The moon was full, high in her course, and all the place was full of her radiance. In the distance the walls of the temple nearest the diamond mountain appeared self-luminous. To that the guide walked, and we reached the door now standing wide open. As I came to the threshold, suddenly the lonely, grey, wandering eye of my old dead friend and co-disciple floated past looking deep into my own, and I read its expression as if it would say:

"The picture gallery is here."

We entered, and, although some priests were there, no one seemed to notice me. Through a court, across a hall, down a long corridor we went, and then into a wide and high roofless place with but one door. Only the stars in heaven adorned the space above, while streams of more than moonlight poured into it from the diamond, so that there were no shadows nor any need for lights. As the noiseless door swung softly to behind us, sad music floated down the place and ceased; just then a sudden shadow seemed to grow in one spot, but was quickly swallowed in the light.

"Examine with care, but touch not and fear nothing," said my taciturn cicerone. With these words he turned and left me alone.

But how could I say I was alone? The place was full of faces. They were ranged up and down the long hall; near the floor, above it, higher, on the walls, in the air, everywhere except in one aisle, but not a single one moved from its place, yet each was seemingly alive. And at intervals strange watchful creatures of the elemental world that moved about from place to place. Were they watching me or the faces? Now I felt they had me in view, for sudden glances out of the corners of their eyes shot my way; but in a moment something happened showing they guarded or watched the faces.

I was standing looking at the face of an old friend about my own age who had been sent to another part of the island, and it filled me with sadness unaccountably. One of the curious elemental creatures moved silently up near it. In amazement I strained my eyes, for the picture of my friend was apparently discoloring. Its expression altered every moment. It turned from white to grey and yellow, and back to grey, and then suddenly it grew all black as if with rapid decomposition. Then again that same sad music I had heard on entering floated past me, while the blackness of the face seemed to cast a shadow, but not long. The elemental pounced upon the blackened face now soulless, tore it in pieces, and by some process known to itself dissipated the atoms and restored the brightness of the spot. But alas! my old friend's picture was gone, and I felt within me a heavy, almost unendurable gloom as of despair.

As I grew accustomed to the surroundings, my senses perceived every now and then sweet but low musical sounds that appeared to emanate from or around these faces. So, selecting one, I stood in front of it and watched. It was bright and pure. Its eyes looked into mine with the half-intelligence of a dream. Yes, it grew now and then a little brighter, and as that happened I heard the gentle music. This convinced me that the changes in expression were connected with the music.

But fearing I would be called away, I began to carefully scan the collection, and found that all my co-disciples were represented there, as well as hundreds whom I had never seen, and every priest high or low whom I had observed about the island. Yet the same saddening music every now and then reminded me of the scene of the blackening of my friend's picture. I knew it meant others blackened and being destroyed by the watchful elementals who I could vaguely perceive were pouncing upon something whenever those notes sounded. They were like the wails of angels when they see another mortal going to moral suicide.

Dimly after a while there grew upon me an explanation of this gallery. Here were the living pictures of every student or priest of the order founded by the Adepts of the Diamond Mountain. These vitalized pictures were connected by invisible cords with the character of those they represented, and like a telegraph instrument they instantly recorded the exact state of the disciple's mind; when he made a complete failure, they grew black and were destroyed; when he progressed in spiritual life, their degrees of brightness or beauty showed his exact standing. As these conclusions were reached, louder and stronger musical tones filled the hall. Directly before me was a beautiful, peaceful face; its brilliance outshone the light around, and I knew that some unseen brother — how far or near was unknown to me — had reached some height of advancement that corresponded to such tones. Just then my guide re-entered; I found I was near the door; it was open, and together we passed out, retracing the same course by which we had entered. Outside again the setting of the moon showed how long I had been in the gallery. The silence of my guide prevented speech, and he returned with me to the room I had left. There he stood looking at me, and once more I heard as it were from afar his voice in inquiry, as if he said but,

"Well?"

Into my mind came the question "How are those faces made?" From all about him, but not from his lips, came the answer,

"You cannot understand. They are not the persons, and yet they are made from their minds and bodies."

"Was I right in the idea that they were connected with those they pictured by invisible cords along which the person's condition was carried?"

"Yes, perfectly. And they never err. From day to day they change for better or for worse. Once the disciple has entered his path his picture forms there; and we need no spies, no officious fellow disciples to prefer charges, no reports, no machinery. Everything registers itself. We have but to inspect the images to know just how the disciple gets on or goes back."

"And those curious elementals," thought I, "do they feed on the blackened images?"

"They are our scavengers. They gather up and dissipate the decomposed and deleterious atoms that formed the image before it grew black — no longer fit for such good company."

"And the music, — did it come from the images?"

"Ah, boy, you have much to learn. It came from them, but it belongs also to every other soul. It is the vibration of the disciple's thoughts and spiritual life; it is the music of his good deeds and his brotherly love."

Then there came to me a dreadful thought, "How can one — if at all — restore his image once it has blackened in the gallery?"

But my guide was no longer there. A faint rustling sound was all — and three deep far notes as if upon a large bronze bell!

The Path, June 1889   **BRYAN KINNAVAN**
                                         (W.Q. JUDGE)

Deeds of sacrifice, of mortification, and of charity are not to be abandoned, for they are proper to be performed, and are the purifiers of the wise. But even those works are to be performed after having renounced all selfish interest in them and in their fruit.

THE PYTHAGOREAN SANGHA

THE JEWEL IN THE LOTUS edited by Raghavan Iyer

THE GRIHASTHA ASHRAMA by B. P. Wadia

THE MORAL AND POLITICAL THOUGHT
OF MAHATMA GANDHI by Raghavan Iyer

THE BHAGAVAD GITA edited by Raghavan Iyer

THE MAITREYA ACADEMY

PARAPOLITICS — TOWARD THE CITY OF MAN by Raghavan Iyer

THE PLATONIC QUEST by E. J. Urwick

OBJECTIVITY AND CONSCIOUSNESS by Robert Rein'l

SANGAM TEXTS

THE BEACON LIGHT by H. P. Blavatsky

THE SERVICE OF HUMANITY by D. K. Mavalankar

HIT THE MARK by W. Q. Judge

THE PROGRESS OF HUMANITY by A. P. Sinnett

CONSCIOUSNESS AND IMMORTALITY by T. Subba Row

THE GATES OF GOLD by M. Collins

THE LANGUAGE OF THE SOUL by R. Crosbie

THE ASCENDING CYCLE by G. W. Russell

THE DOCTRINE OF THE BHAGAVAD GITA by Bhavani Shankar

THE LAW OF SACRIFICE by B. P. Wadia

SACRED TEXTS

RETURN TO SHIVA (from the *Yoga Vasishtha Maharamayana*)

THE GATHAS OF ZARATHUSTRA — The Sermons of Zoroaster

TAO TE CHING by Lao Tzu

SELF-PURIFICATION (Jaina Sutra)

THE DIAMOND SUTRA (from the Final Teachings of the Buddha)

THE GOLDEN VERSES OF PYTHAGORAS
    (with the commentary of Hierocles)

IN THE BEGINNING — The Mystical Meaning of Genesis

THE GOSPEL ACCORDING TO THOMAS
    (with complementary texts)

THE SEALS OF WISDOM — The Essence of Islamic Mysticism
    by Ibn al-'Arabi

CHANTS FOR CONTEMPLATION by Guru Nanak

INSTITUTE OF WORLD CULTURE

THE SOCIETY OF THE FUTURE by Raghavan Iyer

THE RELIGION OF SOLIDARITY by Edward Bellamy

THE BANQUET (Percy Bysshe Shelley's translation
    of Plato's *Symposium*)

THE DREAM OF RAVAN *A Mystery*

THE LAW OF VIOLENCE AND THE LAW OF LOVE by Leo Tolstoy

THE RECOVERY OF INNOCENCE by Pico Iyer

UTILITARIANISM AND ALL THAT by Raghavan Iyer

NOVUS ORDO SECLORUM by Raghavan Iyer

The CGP emblem identifies this book as a production of Concord Grove Press, publishers since 1975 of books and pamphlets of enduring value in a format based upon the Golden Ratio. This volume was typeset in Journal Roman Bold, printed and softbound by Sangam Printers. A list of publications can be obtained from Concord Grove Press, P.O. Box 959, Santa Barbara, California 93102, U.S.A.